A SAï Lïï World...?

Luc Debieuvre

With a Foreword by
Abdul Hamid, Editor-In-Chief of the *Gulf News*

South Street Press

A SAFER WORLD …?

Published by
South Street Press
8 Southern Court
South Street
Reading
RG1 4QS
UK
www.southstreetpress.co.uk

South Street Press is an imprint of Garnet Publishing Limited.

Copyright © Luc Debieuvre 2007

All rights reserved.
No part of this book may be reproduced in any form or by any electronic or mechanical means, including information storage and retrieval systems, without permission in writing from the publisher, except by a reviewer who may quote brief passages in a review.

First Edition

ISBN-13: 978-0-86372-310-0
ISBN-10: 0-86372-310-1

British Library Cataloguing-in-Publication Data
A catalogue record for this book is available from the British Library.

Typeset by Samantha Barden.
Jacket design by David Rose.
Cover photograph reproduced with permission of Peter Turnley/Corbis.

Printed by Biddles, UK.

Who can deny that we now live in a safer world …?
George W. Bush

Contents

About the author   viii
Foreword   ix
Introduction: Two years later …   1

2003
A Year of Lies

6 March	Matter of autonomy and that of survival	7
24 March	Big Brother gives rise to new colonial power	11
7 April	Rest of the world have lost their love for the US	15
24 April	Palestine a promised land, yes … but to whom?	19
28 April	Unlike diamonds, Mr Safire's words are not forever	23
8 May	EU must develop its own policies	25
27 May	Neo-conservatives do not typify the US	29
9 June	Ties can't be based upon subordination	33
23 June	War of words has now begun	37
7 July	War and terrorism: never the twain should mix	41
20 July	Speaking the truth helps to build mutual understanding	45
5 August	The seven mortal sins of American blindness	49
17 August	Europe versus America?	53
1 September	No super-power, however mighty, rules the world alone	57
15 September	US's misguided foreign policies expose its political juvenility	61
29 September	Time to offer Sharon a one-way ticket	65
13 October	Europe's choice: to be a power or remain a vassal	69
28 October	Why is the world so bad?	73
10 November	A farewell to law	77
24 November	Will the US allow Europe to become an adult?	81
8 December	Time to get rid of the plague of neo-colonial democracy	85

22 December	World headlines: either too sweet or too sour	89

2004
OLD WARS, NEW WARS

5 January	A year all out of lies, lies and more lies	95
18 January	When it comes to transparency	99
2 February	Headscarf scare creates a new law in France	103
16 February	"Upon the wall, I write your name, Freedom"	107
1 March	One may prefer democrats to smoking guns	111
15 March	Bush has not achieved his job	115
9 April	Sharon will continue to attack	117
13 April	Taking the wrong approach towards democracy	121
26 April	The use of force will lead to nowhere	125
10 May	There's need to pilot US plane before it crashes	129
24 May	Daily horrors must not stop the looking forward	133
7 June	Narrow is the road to democracy in the Middle East	137
21 June	Is American democracy heading towards tyranny?	141
5 July	What is sovereignty when the US controls Iraq?	145
19 July	If not Israel, who makes the world more dangerous?	149
2 August	Turkey's admission to EU is a matter of grave concern	153
16 August	What's a new transatlantic alliance for?	157
30 August	Sharon's expansionism contravenes international law	161
13 September	Legacy of a "war president" is nothing to be proud of	165
27 September	Posing wrong questions about a true crisis	169
11 October	Fighting an enemy without identifying it first	173
25 October	Europe and the US should form a symbiotic relationship	177
3 November	France has lost a very close friend	181
8 November	Dollar is sinking as deficit mounts	183
22 November	Nothing has changed with Arafat's death	187

6 December	There is no exit strategy for the United States in Iraq	191
20 December	French rift with the US could spread across Europe	195

2005
WORKING FOR A FUTURE

3 January	Kind wishes alone will not be enough for the New Year	201
17 January	Abu Mazen's balancing act in Palestine	205
31 January	America may lose the war … or maybe it already has	209
16 February	Iraq's worsening situation may be good for Palestine	213
28 February	A change in tone won't do the trick	217
14 March	Time is running out in the Middle East	221
28 March	The buck stops with Damascus	225
11 April	Sowing the seeds of the third intifada	229
25 April	Moment of truth for the French	233
9 May	Europe must come to the aid of Syria	237

Index 241

ABOUT THE AUTHOR

Luc Debieuvre is a French national who lives in Paris and travels frequently to the Middle East, where he has also been posted. A law graduate (Panthéon Sorbonne, Sciences Po), he spent his career in banking, most recently as head of an Arab bank in Paris. Between 2003 and 2005, he wrote fortnightly chronicles for the UAE-based *Gulf News*, one of the most influential English-language Arab dailies in the Gulf. He is also a board member of the Institute for International and Strategic Research (IRIS), a Paris-based think-tank.

Foreword

A mutual friend approached me in 2003 saying that Luc Debieuvre was interested in writing a column for *Gulf News*. On asking about his background I was informed he was a banker, not a journalist.

I was surprised. Not surprised because a Frenchman wanted to write for an English-language newspaper published in the Arabian Gulf, but because here was an accomplished and well-known banker, keen to analyse and comment on international affairs and politics, and not just limit his writing to finance and economics.

Accustomed to receiving such requests from journalists, academics and columnists, I was intrigued by Luc's offer and decided to take him up on it. In the post-9/11 world, global politics and the relationships between East and West, North and South, rich and poor, Christianity and Islam, have been in a state of flux. To my mind, someone unconnected with the media establishment and looking at the issues from a different perspective could bring freshness and clarity to the opinion pages of *Gulf News*.

That judgment was spot-on. In his columns published in *Gulf News* over a period of 18 months, Luc Debieuvre fostered a lively debate and commented on the issues of the day in an inimitable and incisive manner. Not subscribing to stereotypical views and beliefs, he enlarged the debate by exploring different avenues of thought and brought a uniquely European flavour to the table. His writing stimulated discussion and prompted considerable reader interest, as evidenced by the large number of people who wrote in to the newspaper in response.

The period of Luc's association with *Gulf News* has been among the most significant and memorable in recent history. The aftermath of America's War on Terror that brought in its wake the events in Afghanistan and the continuing misadventure in Iraq has unleashed forces that the world will have to contend with and endure well after the protagonists have left the stage. Perhaps it was these events and the West's motivations in driving them that motivated Luc Debieuvre to comment on these matters.

The continuing turmoil in the Middle East, the Palestinian struggle and the impact of this volatile region on the global economy will undoubtedly continue in the months and years to come and I hope Luc Debieuvre will continue to analyse and unravel their intricacies in the future.

In this book, an attempt has been made to collate and present to readers in one convenient package 18 months of Luc's writings in *Gulf News*. In this laudable venture I wish him all success.

Abdul Hamid Ahmad
Editor-In-Chief
Gulf News
Dubai, United Arab Emirates

INTRODUCTION: TWO YEARS LATER ...

A fortnightly chronicle provides a much better opportunity than a daily commentary to look at an event with some distance, placing it within a wider reasoning process which can help us to understand it while simultaneously linking it to the current course of events. The republishing of such chronicles would therefore be nothing more than the recording of an instant testimony, something weighted with the feeling of the moment and, at best, a possible source of information for future historians wishing to explain how a specific event was understood or analysed the day it took place.

Why, then, should these fifty-two articles be gathered together in the same book, if they were intended only to be current reactions in which interest would disappear as the underlying events pass by?

There may be many explanations, not least the basic difference that exists between a book and a newspaper. Books survive, whereas time seems to consume newspapers. Any author willing to see the insuperable heights of his thoughts engraved forever in the marble of a written testimony aimed at future generations will opt for a book. It is the cheapest way to satisfy an ego, and authors have egos. But, more seriously, there are two main reasons to proceed this way.

First, a succession of apparently different events may constitute the sequences of a single major event that ultimately becomes defined by all these developments and latest outcomes. It puts itself within a wider context progressively defined by such input. As an example, each chronicle devoted to a specific aspect of the Israeli–Palestinian conflict becomes an element of a more global history about the Palestinian fight for freedom. Each article is linked to another one and helps to describe a global situation, explain a cause and foresee a likely future. The virtue of repeating should not be forgotten either. "The only democracy in the Middle East", as some people like to name it, practises a continued violence which tends to go unnoticed, precisely because it continues. It is therefore important to show it relentlessly, to denounce it again and again, and never to allow good feeling people to fall asleep with the insurance of their own conscience being at peace, simply because they are unable to do anything about it and eventually become accustomed to it.

Second, a columnist is someone who takes a risk – intellectually, at least. It is true to say that sometimes these risks seem to be rather safe ones, as few people tend to remind us what was said of an event a few months after it occurred. A well-known French analyst, now heading one of the major French think-tanks, made himself notorious when he predicted that former President Bush Senior would never intervene in the Gulf. Another analyst, who writes weekly apparently unbiased chronicles on any historical or political matter in the French daily *Le Figaro*, did even better when predicting both that Bush Junior would not invade Iraq and that Senator John Kerry would win the presidential election. Back to a not-so-distant past, I'm also reminded of the cover page of the French daily *Le Monde*, dated 30 April 1975: "In Phnom Penh, a cheering crowd welcomes its liberators." After such an exploit, any outside observer would feel some kind of embarrassment and could think that a certain dignity would commend them to keep quiet for a while, or at least to apologise to their readers. After all, who doesn't make mistakes? But some people don't; they continue to write and tell the world their version of the truth. This is a rather common practice in countries like France, where people are divided between the official thinkers, and the rest. The so-called intellectuals and other official specialists know what they are talking about, by definition. They hardly accept dissonance; look at the furore that accompanied the publishing of Pascal Boniface's (founder and director of IRIS) book *Est-il permis de critiquer Israël?* (Are we allowed to criticize Israel?) (Editions Robert Laffont, 2003). Dr Boniface, a former adviser for international affairs of the French Socialist Party (PS), wrote an internal note and then later a book about the Israeli–Palestinian conflict. He fell victim of a truly organized campaign against him in the press on the grounds of anti-Semitic behaviour.

As for members of the "civil society", they are kindly requested to stand by and keep quiet. Yet reading, listening, exchanging views and experience is something that can easily occur in addition to a daily professional occupation. In this respect, it has been a great honour, indeed a great pleasure, that *Gulf News* has readily welcomed my columns. But it has been an even greater satisfaction to see that many of my earlier comments, analyses and predictions, have proven, with time, to be true – however unfortunate in some cases. The American war in Iraq has been a terrible example in this respect. We never gave credit to the false reasons put forward to justify a pre-emptive war by an administration which had already made its decision; we hardly believed that the Americans would be welcome as liberators by the population as a whole, especially if they were about to stay for a while; we could not imagine that the war would be over in June 2003 nor that the US could end it with its currently available forces; most importantly, we did not accept the concept of unilateralism, not because it would be arrogant and counter-productive, but because we found it fundamentally inefficient. "They can make the war alone but they will need the rest of the world to make the peace," French President Jacques Chirac said at the time. The present situation in Iraq is no reason for satisfaction, the famous "I told you so". But it is no reason either to keep quiet just because one has been proven right. In the 2003 autumn issue of the French magazine *Politique Internationale*, Amin Taheri explained, one by one, the reasons why the US was legally authorised to go to war in Iraq and why the war was going to be a success. The reasons were false and the results are what we know. At the same time, other people held different conclusions, and they were right. A year and a half later, this book is a tribute to them.

Among the most debilitating ideas put forward by George W. Bush's first administration, the concept of the "Broader Middle East initiative" takes the lead. Imposing democracy by force, starting an election process when people have no work, no food and no security, lining up each and everybody along the same Western pattern supposed to be the world standard, deciding on behalf of others what is good or bad for them – all this is simply stupid and arrogant. But, more importantly, it can have devastating effects upon those in the region who have been working step by step towards democracy – a reasonable march, unhurried and suiting local characteristics, enabling the concept to take its roots genuinely. Besides those rulers in the United Arab Emirates, Qatar and elsewhere who are the new political pioneers of the Arab world, one institution can play a major role in the implementation of democracy so much better than Mrs Condoleezza Rice's ukases: the press. Therefore, before readers return to the chronicles collected in this book and let their imaginations work again, let me tell them how bright some futures may be in the region as long as institutions like *Gulf News* continue to work the way they have done thus far.

My thanks go not just to this institution but to all those who play an outstanding role in offering freedom of speech and promoting democracy.

Luc Debieuvre, July 2005

2003
A YEAR OF LIES

Timeline World News 2003

21 January:	France and Germany declare they are opposed to any war in Iraq.
27 January:	Baghdad refuses to accept disarmament.
14 February:	UN inspectors say they can't find any banned arms in Iraq.
27 February:	Iraq claims it will destroy its missiles.
1 March:	The Arab League makes public that it opposes war in Iraq.
15 March:	There are rallies across the world in protest at an impending war in Iraq.
17 March:	US President George W. Bush tells Saddam Hussein that he has 48 hours to leave Iraq, or there will be a military invasion.
19 March:	Saddam Hussein does not leave. The US enter war with Iraq.
4 April:	US troops break into Baghdad.
9 April:	US forces gain control of Baghdad.
1 May:	Bush delivers televised address calling for an end to major combat in Iraq.
16 June:	The UK begins an enquiry into the so-called weapons of mass destruction.
3 July:	Massive reward offered to Iraq by US for the capture of Saddam Hussein.
22 July:	Saddam Hussein's sons killed after their hideout in Mosul is revealed.
August:	UN Secretary Koffi Anan issues several critical statements about the conduct of the war in Iraq by the US.
29 August:	Ayatollah Mohammad Baqir al-Hakim, the spiritual leader of the Supreme Council for Islamic Revolution, is killed in a bomb blast at Azzamiya mosque, Baghdad.
1 November:	US says Iraqi handover to be speeded up.
3 November:	Blasts hits Baghdad Green Zone. US Congress says budget for Iraq is OK.
Fall 2003:	For the first time, the EU plans and conducts military operations without recourse to NATO resources and capabilities in Macedonia and DR Congo.
14 December:	Saddam Hussein is captured.

MATTER OF AUTONOMY AND THAT OF SURVIVAL

6 March 2003

The United States of America decided on it, and we are now contemplating the apparently unavoidable arrival of a war that this country wanted, and which was not imposed on it.

Throughout time, philosophers have endlessly discussed war, its possible legitimacy or absolute rejection. Other generations will pass on before a unanimous world defines what would be a just war. Others, who considered as a starting point war as an unavoidable phenomenon, have preferred to think of what could be the best way to win it. A supreme art has been to avoid war altogether. This in a certain way is what has underpinned the action of France these last months.

But how could one stick to these considerations when, in a horribly practical manner, France will have to take a position on the use of its right of veto at the Security Council: only those who don't play cards do not see the inanity of such debate. While this right does not have any meaning other than the one to exercise a threat, it puts whoever uses it into one or the other camp once the threat is executed. More simply, the question is to know whether France should or should not support the war, and those who make it.

A first anecdotal answer would be to say that since those who do not hesitate to fence off their country's policy in the columns of the *Wall Street Journal* recommend supporting it, it is vital to hold on.

With discussion among the political left being reduced to "No to war" because it is war, or "No to war" because on top of that it is a war against the Arabs, it lacks consistency. In a parallel reasoning, it would be "Yes to war" because Iraq is a danger for Israel. But Israel is also a danger for Palestine and, despite the fact that Israel has not respected the hundreds of resolutions voted for by the United Nations since 1967 compelling it to free the territories it has occupied in an illegitimate way through the use of force (there are no more than 18 resolutions relating to Iraq today), one hasn't yet gone to war against Israel. On the contrary, discussions go on, moving forward as in Oslo or backward as with Ariel Sharon. It is obvious that war against Iraq has no factual justification, unless a new international law on intervention is decided on – the practical aspects of which would be nothing less than the opinion of the most powerful. Other dictators, unfortunately, oppress their people. Other states, unfortunately, go on representing a serious threat to the international community, and still the whole world is not permanently at war with them. Other elements thus led the United States to decide on that war: a declining relationship with Saudi Arabia, a willingness to control immense oil resources or to preach a new crusade, which used to be called a "colonial war". However, isn't the true question for us Europeans of a different nature? Are we not on the verge of reliving the Suez crisis of 1956, being alone at this time in front of the United States? And wouldn't the war against Iraq be a simple lure when tolls the knell of Europe?

Indeed, what can the position of France be today and which space can be saved for it in the near future? One knows the international context. On the one hand, there are many of those countries which think that they cannot have the luxury of a completely independent policy and have no choice but to rely on the support of others, especially that of the United States. On the other hand, one also knows more or less the position of the Arab states in the region. Besides those whose freedom of speech is inversely proportional to the cover of their budget by the United States, many of these states are embarrassed by the position of France. Beyond an apparent solidarity, these states are managed by a governing minority elite who, for various reasons, decided long ago to stand by the United States, whereas public opinion, the so-called "Arab street", becomes increasingly Islamic with each day that passes along the rhythm of Israeli exactions, thinking that aggression against an Arab entity is aggression against Islam. Most cleverly governed states in the region sail between these two reefs, fully aware of their limited room for manoeuvre. At least France, when in the Atlantic bosom, used to represent a nuance if not an alternative. In the case of total victory by the United States, France's present position means it risks isolating itself in the region.

That said, the alternative is no more heartening. If victory by the United States is not total and military operations last longer than expected, or if there is an explosion of terrorist acts in the Middle East or worldwide, or if extremist Islam strengthens to the point that it may become a governing power in some countries, France's situation is still no better. Some Arab states in the region justify their support of the United States under the pretext of the existence of a link between Iraq and Al Qaida: no honest observer can imagine any such link between Islamic fundamentalists and a substitute of exotic Stalinism. An explosion of fanaticism following the inception of a war in Iraq cannot be seen as a fantastic notion. The alternative for France would thus reduce it to following the United States in their crusade – probably in the uncomfortable situation of a last-minute alliance – or to pride itself on its virtue as a third world headlight of multipolarity, and peacefully wait for Islamic forces to gain power, although these will not respect it either.

Avoiding such extremes has been a driving force of our diplomacy in recent months, but deadlines get closer. And a graceful exit through Europe seems to be the only way to break this false logic imposed by the United States. When French industry is still wondering whether it has a chance to secure an arms supply contract in the region without realising the extent to which issues have changed, it is high time we distanced ourselves from that zone in order to return to the central point this war in Iraq would try and hide – that is, the nature of the relationship between Europe and the United States. The question for France is relatively simple: is it in its interest that a strong Europe develops, even though it opposes, albeit peacefully, other existing forces? Great Britain showed that a different choice could be made, which can be perfectly justified so long as one knows which camp one sits in. If the United States have worked so hard in recent months to divide Europe, this is precisely because they prefer to deal with isolated and smaller partners than with a united and consequently stronger partner. We like the United States and haven't forgotten the links we have with them. However, we may also have diverting interests, and we alone will be less and less in a position to protect them. This is why this war has revealed so much about international relationships in Europe, as we shall soon witness. A hardly born political union is already dead. It should thus be created again, on a fair basis this time, starting with a limited nucleus of states – Germany, Belgium, France, The Netherlands – that are prepared to agree on the main issues. It is a matter of autonomy, and thus of survival. This in order that a new Suez doesn't put an end to Europe and, in time, to France.

BIG BROTHER GIVES RISE TO NEW COLONIAL POWER

24 MARCH 2003

So they did it. Alone or nearly alone. They claimed to be supported by 80 countries yet hardly a handful is providing them with forces. They said they wanted Iraq to get rid of weapons of mass destruction when they just wanted to get rid of a government they did not like. Their claim that Iraq had re-launched a nuclear programme was denied by the UN Inspectors. Actually, they never gave a chance to peace. A new star has just appeared in the world constellation, a star that will now light up for us, act for us, think for us. It is probably too early to draw conclusions in terms of new post-Cold War equilibrium. Unfortunately, it is not too late to inform you that a new colonial power is born.

In making decisions on its own, the American government has tainted democracy for everyone, violated international law and paved the way for tyranny. Because France helped them to create a nation 250 years ago, America believed they were the only ones to understand democracy. It seems some teaching may still be needed. Democracy starts when you respect others. It normally goes with votes. Thus, one cannot say that "diplomacy collapsed" because it did not win a majority of votes. The UN Security Council did not have a majority on the US proposal to lead war against Iraq. A majority was not there, and a result cannot be considered as "unreasonable" just because it does not fit one's expectations. This is a fact, and going against facts is not a constituting element of democracy. War can be led through many different vehicles; using words is obviously one of them. When Mr Aznar claims that "international law was disrupted by the fact that a resolution authorising war could not be accepted by the UN Security Council", he is distorting facts. British Prime Minister Tony Blair was acting in a similar way when he shamelessly declared that "the only way to preserve peace was to vote for the US-sponsored resolution", which was nothing else but an authorisation for war. Everybody knows the old Roman saying "*Si vis pacem para bellum* [If you want peace, prepare yourself for war]".

In the language of America, this has become "If you want peace, vote for war".

A legal war is a war that is made by a country in a move of self-defence, or that is authorised by the United Nations. This is the basis of international relationships, and this is the reason why the United States have been trying to obtain a resolution from the UN authorising them to lead war in Iraq. They would not have looked for it if they did not need it. But as they could not obtain it, they said they did not need it. This is not a lack of democracy; this is cheating. The fact that Saddam Hussein cheated as well is not justification enough: when one goes on using the same petty means as one's enemy, tyranny is not far away.

And precisely, tyranny starts when whoever is accused of a crime has to prove first that he is not guilty. Democracy works the other way round. But America did not prove anything. Tyranny is also when people start thinking on your behalf. As everyone knows, an Arab state has just been put up for sale. Not one of the states that has already sold itself for money and that is prevented from being put up for sale again. But we are now talking of Iraq, which Americans have indeed just put on their buying list. Yet, force will say that this is a restrictive sale: only American companies are invited to bid. As *Wall Street Journal* put it:

> By going it alone, the US will open a new chapter in nation building ... they will do everything, from repairing Iraqi roads, schools and hospitals to revamping its financial rules and government payroll systems.

Big Brother will even think for you. Has George Orwell not been translated from English into American?

But this is not the worst of it. This conflict, as the new crusaders put it, "marks shift from the containment of enemies to pre-emption". When the sole super-power claims the right to launch pre-emptive war, at will, one can be seriously anxious. As an analyst, Martin Wolf, put it in a deliciously worded understatement: "Breaching the legitimacy of the UN and putting a premium on the use of force over the rule of law is to assume a heavy responsibility." Indeed, especially when all this is relying upon the sagacity of Bush Junior and his friends. Arrogance linked to the faith of the newly converted seems to lead them in a major wrong direction: the belief that after they intervene, a magic wand will turn Iraq and other countries in the region into liberal democracies. That said, who can now feel safe? Surely not other dictatorships elsewhere, which may be good, but also those who do not share the Bush Administration view of democracy or what is suitable for people. For instance, whom does America have in mind when it says that the new developments in Iraq will allow for "other serious changes in the region"? With some sense of irony, it could happen that those states who were the strongest supporters of the United States could be the ones who will be forced to change leadership first.

Needless to say, it is furthermore hardly possible to trust the American government when it tells its would-be followers that the situation will now evolve in Palestine. How, indeed, could anybody seriously believe that a coalition of activist Jews together with fundamentalist Protestants will take the future of the Palestinian people into consideration? This would be as sensible as saying to the Palestinian people that they will now be protected from Ariel Sharon's actions by the Spanish army.

Now that war has begun and that every sensible human hopes it will not last, people will start to reflect on what has happened. Indeed, nobody is a supporter of the regime of Saddam Hussein, and what Iraqis are about to suffer may be little compared to what they have suffered over the last 20 years. Who would not feel concerned for the Iraqi people? But besides the unpredictable internal and external consequences of an illegal armed action, a major concern remains the right given to a super-power to impose edicts all over the world and decide by itself what is good or not. France (and many others countries) tried to oppose that vision of international law. It was dragged through the mud by an unbelievable campaign of hate from the Anglo-Saxon camp. The words heard on that occasion were actually of little importance; as for the jokes made at their expense, the French usually do not understand them. As long as "Freedom" fries are made the same way as "French" fries and Inspector Colombo keeps his exhausted Peugeot car, life will go on. These negative words are only a reflection of the uncomfortable and lonely situation in which the new reduced coalition now stands. More worrying could be the concerted action of the various media means of the Murdoch empire, because it is another side of emerging and growing hegemonic attitudes in our world. Yet, as long as we know who they are working for, this should be kept under control. Actually, the French are not angry; they are simply appalled. They do not fear any US retaliatory measures against them after the war in Iraq, because war itself is the result of the new relationship emerging between America and Europe. As a French analyst, Guillaume Parmentier, a Professor at the Law University in Paris, recently wrote:

> Weakening the security council, dividing NATO and splitting the European Union – the three institutions on which the US has built its foreign policy for the last five years – would prove a very heavy price to pay to get rid of a tinpot dictator. (*Politique Internationale*, Winter 2002).

"God Bless America!" They need it.

REST OF THE WORLD HAVE LOST THEIR LOVE FOR THE US

7 April 2003

A favourite game among analysts these days is to try to predict what will happen next in the region once the war is over. A major problem, however, is that all analysis depends on so many conflicting hypotheses that it has become possible to predict almost anything and everything.

An obvious example is the outcome of the war itself. A starting (and indisputable) point for consideration is the ill-conceived strategy of the Bush Administration, according to which both the efficiency of used weapons and spontaneous friendly welcome for the liberators by the population would have led Saddam Hussein's regime to collapse within a few days. The only element taken for granted is that, thanks to America and the arrogant Donald Rumsfeld, the despotic leader Saddam Hussein is on the way to martyrdom – not to mention a likely worldwide rise in terrorism, a dramatic economic slowdown and a clear perception that war, which is not a video game, will cost hundreds of millions of dollars and yet achieve little more than the refinancing of American companies, through their winning of reconstruction contracts.

Yet, the way analysts predicted a seven-day war sharply contrasted with questions they seemed to ask openly last week about America's capacity to win. War was won before it started, and it would be lost when it had hardly started. We continue to have no doubt about the final issue, yet the harm is done. Scenes of absolute despair, wounded children and jammed hospitals, together with pictures of civilians searched by the US army, mean that the traditional image of the American soldier will be spoilt for a long time. Furthermore, whatever happens next? Who will reasonably believe that America will now be able to run Iraq? Even though, in a last-ditch effort, they would not pursue the Rumsfeld plans to set up a Mafia-type management of the country, they will have to take Arab pride into consideration if they do not want to fight one billion Muslims.

For the rest, commenting on the future of each country in the region is like saying that if things go well, then everything will go well, and the other way round. One may prefer to keep one's head above these troubled waters and start to concentrate on the actual issue of tomorrow: not the way Iraq should be managed nor "taken to private" as Robert McFarlane, Head of the US National Security Council, wrote in the *Wall Street Journal*. One may simply enquire: how do we now want the world to be managed and world affairs led? In that respect, two very opposite views are emerging.

On the one hand, countries led by the Bush Administration believe that the world is in disorder, and that this should be firmly corrected with appropriate measures. This is a logic of strength, of "willingness" against the "unwilling". There is no room for doubt in the fight between "who has guts and who has not", as the Murdoch press might write. America was attacked on 11 September 2001. It had to defend itself with the help of its friends, and those who are not with it are against it. Unfortunately, these are many: there's the "axis of evil", of course, but there are also other places where local policies do not fit with what the Bush Administration thinks is good for them. This is why, as Colin Powell put it, "it is possible that a success in Iraq allows for fundamentally reshaping this region in a positive way, which also progresses American interest". More than the quest for oil, which cannot be totally denied when so many internal reports have insisted over the last years on "an absolute necessity for the US to secure a better access to oil reserves", this is, we believe, the underlying attitude of the Bush Administration's involvement in Iraq – and tomorrow elsewhere.

The only problem is that world affairs are more complex, and simple logic doesn't always apply. For instance, is it worth reminding ourselves that Osama bin Laden probably did more against the US with a couple of knives than any other country with more sophisticated weapons? And what did US-sponsored regulations on money laundering do in the fight against terrorism, when one knows that a few stolen credit cards used in automatic teller machines provide enough cash to organise an attempt such as the one on the USS *Cole*? In other words, is not the "pure strength" attitude somewhat archaic in today's world?

This question goes far beyond whether the transatlantic rift between the US and Europe should be repaired, or if the UN should play a role tomorrow in Iraq. The American Marines will not run Iraq after the war, and they are not ruling Afghanistan either. Sticking solely to the Iraqi problem is like keeping one's nose over a bicycle handlebar. Today's world is diversified and complex, and future situations will probably become increasingly complex. It is also becoming increasingly dangerous; new crises will emerge and the world will have to find new solutions for them. Some countries believe the world is so disorganised that one should make the utmost effort to avoid disorganising it further, and so escape the unnecessary shocks and confrontations. This doesn't rule out the principle of war provided it is authorised by the recognised international institution, which is the United Nations. It may also require new ideas, such as creating a new corps to disarm international forces or a new corps of human rights soldiers. But above all it implies a logic of co-operation, of working together. In a multilateral approach, there is an ability to build bridges, to maintain contacts between different entities, to gain from the experience and, finally, to make people draw nearer. As the French Minister for Foreign Affairs D. de Villepin recently put it, "It is time to generate a positive logic and, beyond past declarations or irritation created by unnecessary bad words, rediscover the virtues of diplomacy." This is not utopia, but human respect and a contribution to a better organised world.

The future of Europe lies within these lines. Actors willing to have their views taken into consideration will have better chances to do so if they are stronger rather than weaker, especially when dealing with a single super-power. The question is whether Europe should simply be an ally of the US within a transatlantic alliance, with the right to talk but with no real decision-making power, or, on the contrary, to exist by itself and in so doing be a sort of counterweight to America or to any other future hegemonic powers. The UK made a choice of its own, which is perfectly defendable. However, other countries may prefer to reinforce existing structures and, through a multispeed process, lean towards a so-called "core Europe", as Belgium is proposing when inviting Germany, Luxembourg and France to join a defence summit in Brussels next week. On the other hand, building Europe doesn't mean going to war with the United States: economies are mixing in a growing manner, industrial and financial flows make barriers disappear. (Incidentally, it was enough to remind the Bush Administration that 650,000 American citizens work for French-owned companies to forget about a serious boycott.) But why couldn't Europe express its own vision of the world, its own values, its own approach to other people, other cultures? As Villepin said: "The West must come together to face the common threats ... The new US strategic doctrines of primacy without constraint, and preventive wars fought by a coalition of the willing, have engendered a new approach of divide and rust." Philip Stephens, a regular contributor is right to add in the *Financial Times* that "France's ambitions for a multipolar world in which the US too is constrained by the rule of international law is unachievable for as long as Europe is fractured". Thus, why not start immediately putting back together whoever wants to be put together? For the rest, America may win the war, but they've already lost "hearts and spirits".

PALESTINE A PROMISED LAND, YES ... BUT TO WHOM?

24 April 2003

At a time when the Bush Administration wants to make the world believe that a coalition of activist Jews and fundamentalist Protestants is now prepared to review the situation in Occupied Palestine, we should be reminded of some basic pieces of truth that subtle propaganda has tended to write off over the years. Actually, the position of the US on Palestine, especially since 11 September 2001, is contrary to both moral and international law. To start with, shouldn't the question of the creation of a Jewish state be raised before the question of the creation of a Palestinian state?

Although nobody is prepared to go backwards, no one can pretend to analyse the current situation without having recourse to history. The creation of the Jewish state in 1948 is a historically dated event, a reappearance of a situation that prevailed wide and large 2000 years ago. Creating again a situation in a world that did not stand still (would anybody seriously consider that Israel was created out of virgin unoccupied lands?) could only be the result of an exceptional event. The exceptional event that justifies the creation of Israel is the Holocaust; and thus the creation of Israel was the price that Europe thought it should pay in order to cleanse itself of a Europe-initiated tragedy. Yet, what is the responsibility of the Palestinian people in the Holocaust?

A community of different people used to live there, a population who could rightfully think that having been there for more than 2000 years, they were at home there. However, the Israelis, in turn, "created" the Palestinians by expelling them from their land and sending them into exile. How could they not feel injustice? The lack of Arab responsibility in the Holocaust, the deep injustice suffered by the Palestinian people, the Israeli occupiers' shamelessness and arrogance and, finally, the maintaining of an old principle of international law that something obtained by force cannot be legally validated, cannot all be ignored. If the Israeli state rightfully thought that it was not safe within the pre-1967 frontiers, the international community should have protected it and answered its legitimate fear about its own survival, but not left it do whatever it wanted, starting with the disrespect of the many resolutions voted against it at the UN which, in a typical example of American duplicity, Colin Powell forgets to mention.

Sooner or later, the Israelis will have to learn how to live together with their neighbours, unless the final choice is one of ethnic purification of the Palestinian people, which Ariel Sharon's policy looks like in close association with the neo-conservative Americans for whom a white Jew who reads the Bible will always be preferred to a bearded Muslim who reads the Holy Qur'an. The Palestinian issue cannot reduce, as the Israeli Professor of Linguistics at Tel Aviv University Tanya Reinhart recently wrote, to "an alternative between doves looking for an apartheid and hawks looking for ethnic purification" (*Israel/Palestine: How to end the war of 1948*, Seven Stories, 2002) especially when, off the record, the main participants agree on these commonly approved parameters:

- the mutual recognition of two states, back to 1967 frontiers with international protection
- a just and agreed resolution on the plight of Palestinian refugees
- the dismantling of illegal Jewish colonies in the Occupied Territories
- the internationalisation of Occupied Jerusalem, revered by the three monotheist religions.

The Oslo process allowed for mutual recognition and confirmed the principle of the creation of two states, but this is some way off. Americans insist today that any progress towards peace should be a prerequisite to any move towards the Palestinians; they have also decided that Yasser Arafat is no longer the right interlocutor. But confining Arafat to his office or invading autonomous territories did not reduce the number of attacks. "Arafat will thus go on being treated as responsible for terrorism even though it is the work of groups which have fought against him for years, and who are spared", wrote the former French affairs minister Hubert Védrine in *Politique Internationale*. Chancelleries will try to substitute Arafat, who was not elegant enough to be perfect, and in the meantime blind terrorism will continue; Osama bin Laden, to whom Palestine is all but a priority issue, will continue to be highly regarded in the Arab Street. Whatever the nature of the link existing between Bin

Laden and Palestine, we carry on thinking. What Americans refuse to acknowledge is that any improvement on the Palestinian issue would start to make Arab public opinion distance itself from Al Qaida or any future followers. On the contrary, maintaining the present US policy will, in the end, come to let demography solve the issue by itself; that will only require a few generations, which is nothing compared to eternity.

The whole of the rest is ridiculous. The current Israeli prime minister, Sharon, is being ridiculous in giving his own definition of terrorism, while the former prime minister, Menachem Begin, took pride in it and used to shell Palestinian villages in the 1930s, voluntarily killing civilians, in order to achieve a political goal.

Richard Perle is being ridiculous using the word "terrorism" whenever action comes from enemies of the US, and "collateral damages" if it comes from themselves. "It is not acceptable to have recourse to the murder of civilians in order to achieve political goals," writes Perle, who in 'The Axis of Evil' in *Politique Internationale*, Spring 2002 is probably alluding to the French Resistance during the Second World War whose members the Germans used to call "terrorists". A bomb over Hiroshima, the psychological impact of which has never been denied, was not terrorism; but a Palestinian who kills an unlawful Israeli settler on his land is a terrorist. When a father causes the bus he drives to explode in a gesture of absolute despair, one cannot deduce that all Palestinians are against the existence of an Israeli state. Worse, this rhetoric is now well established by a diplomacy which, for years, has been blinded by its inability to disclose the links existing between those who took recourse to bombs and those who financed them. Not everything can be explained through "terrorism" which, incidentally, cannot be fought off merely by military means either. As the French General de Gaulle put it: "Israel organises on territories it conquered; an occupation which cannot go on without oppression, repression and expulsion. And a form of resistance develops against it, which it calls terrorism."

US Defence Secretary Donald Rumsfeld is being ridiculous when he argues without blushing that "territories which are occupied by Israel are the result of a war which Israel won in 1967". Thus, strength overcomes law for the American professor of democracy who doesn't hesitate to speak of Israel as "the only democracy in the region" when international law is infringed daily by it in letting illegal colonies take root on Palestinian lands, or which in the Gaza Strip blocked one million Palestinians who live within contact of the 7000 Israelis occupying 30 per cent of the territory.

Finally, all those would-be Islamic teachers are being ridiculous when they learnedly explain that Islam is by definition fanatic, that it is a monolithic block, and that establishing different levels of understanding is at best naive and, at worst criminal. They constantly cite extracts from the Holy Qur'an or use Arabic expressions just to show how smart they are in the same way as Protestant sects cite the Bible every two phrases. Maintaining confusion between racial unrest, North Africa, Palestine and Afghanistan helps would-be Islamic teachers to continue their dirty business instead of, for instance, denouncing the possible links existing, consciously or not, between fanatics and moderates; they had better make sure they read books by Arkoun or Adonis.

In conclusion, the apparently hegemonic position of the US derives from their unrivalled strength, and tends to oppose more and more Europeans who don't always have the means to fulfil their ambitions. This is now evolving into a frontal confrontation and the emergence of a new crusade against the Arab–Islamic world. Explaining 11 September 2001 through the sole effects of the American policy in Palestine would lack as much sense as denying any link between them. Friendship between America and the rest of the world deserves more than an outdated fight between anti-Americanism professionals and sabre-rattling pseudo-crusaders. Palestine, a Promised Land ... yes, but to whom?

UNLIKE DIAMONDS, MR SAFIRE'S WORDS ARE NOT FOREVER

28 April 2003

In these troubled times when a few ignorant people still refuse to be enlightened by the incandescent light of human thinking in our new world, it is good to learn from Mr Safire that the French Republic President Jacques Chirac is fighting for the enterprises of his country to obtain contracts abroad; and why not in Iraq since it would seem that the country was significantly destroyed recently by its liberators? This, of course, is of no concern to US companies, whose altruism and lack of interest for what brings in money is widely known ... especially if such money – gained from Iraqi oil resources – is not theirs.

A great failing of Chirac's is to have opposed "any pressure" on Saddam Hussein to obey UN resolutions. I hope Safire's friends are well aware of what "pressure" means in some Washington circles. As for the "favourite dictator", it is true to say that in this matter France lacks both the experience and address book of our American friends.

More basic than that, it seems Safire does not yet understand that France, Russia, Germany and a few other (52) African plus 116 non-aligned countries still have a problem with that war: it was illegal; it was not agreed by the international community which, sorry Mr Safire, is the UN and not the White House. Both Bush and Blair tried to lure the world with the concept of weapons of mass destruction. But so far they have been unfortunate in being unable to find any (although we all know about the sense of imagination that some special agencies have). We could help our friends in their search to some degree and suggest they start looking where such arms exist for sure in the region – and that is Israel.

A vote at the UN after the war would have helped to ratify this awkward situation. The oil-for-food programme would have been a good pretext. But even that was not to the taste of the new imperialists, as it would have prevented them from doing their own cooking alone. It is normal that arrogance is coupled with greed. But when moral pretension is added to this mix it becomes unbearable. Incidentally, is it not blatant hypocrisy to forget to remind everyone that the US bought probably ten times more oil from Iraq than any other state in the oil-for-food programme, thus generously feeding Saddam Hussein's war chest?

Actually, anything that would prevent the US from managing their own business by themselves – I mean Iraq – is unacceptable to them. General "call-me-Jay" Gardner knows what he is talking about. Maybe this is not the case with Dick Cheney, who surely never heard of Bechtel beforehand. And let's not forget that a "bidding process" is a dangerous step on the way to democracy.

But this is not the worst of it. According to independent sources, Iraq's debt to France is roughly US$1.7 billion. Compare this to the US$2.5 billion worth of Iraqi debts guaranteed by the US Exim Bank. These were mainly contracted in the 1980s when Iraq, then wholly supported by the US, was buying arms from the West in its war against Iran. Mr Safire's ageing memory becomes worrying. He should keep on talking to a poodle; and it seems there are many of them available for adoption these days.

To conclude, there is no need to tell the Arab world what it should think (and, by the way, not the Kurds either who, left abandoned by the US, died for that). Isn't it strange that, these days, everybody on earth is wrong but the US? There are enough wise people in the Arab world able to exert their own judgement. Let's therefore ask them what they think of the way US interests behave in Iraq. "The answer, my friend, is blowing in the wind …"

EU MUST DEVELOP ITS OWN POLICIES

8 May 2003

One month has now elapsed. Saddam Hussein, dead or alive, seems to be out of the picture. The US should be thanked for that. Who would not be satisfied with the demise of a despot? Yet there remains a general feeling of unease among the international community: why does the US victory have such a bitter taste, and why is America becoming an object of fear and rejection?

Maybe it's because of their absolute strength. All dictatorships are fought off through the use of force, but it did not work this time with public opinion. The most powerful country in the world crushes one of the poorest. "Washington has now convinced the world of US military superiority – as if there were any doubters", writes the analyst Dominique Moisi. Yet, should a country launch a pre-emptive war without the agreement of the international community, the price of which is the massacre of the population and the destruction of their resources? The images of the destruction of the Abou Hanifa Mosque in the Azzamiya sector, Baghdad (where US troops led an attack 11 April 2003), of horribly wounded children in hospitals, are not going to vanish easily. The use of strength was not only physical; it had to be global. It has gone beyond diplomatic crushing, the US being resolved to punish all who oppose them, as shown in the words of US Deputy Secretary of Defence Paul Wolfowitz. "France will have to pay the price for its opposition to the war", the worst clichés of xenophobic vulgarity and populist cretinism. Hate was organised, notably with the help of some of the press, with special honours to the *Wall Street Journal* and its Iraqi expert, Amir Taheri. They said France opposed the war because of a special relationship between Jacques Chirac and Saddam Hussein; because of the oil-for-food programme, which would have favoured French enterprise; and finally because Chirac wanted to lead the world. But wasn't the relationship of Donald Rumsfeld and Dick Cheney with the Saddam camp much closer? Didn't the US buy ten times more oil from Iraq than from any other country? If the voice of France was so insignificant, why did they attach so much importance to it? When voices such as those of the French Minister for Foreign Affairs are given a standing ovation in the UN by 52 African and 116 non-aligned countries, isn't the free world shifting camp? France and its partners actually opposed the war because it was illegal, based on lies, duplicity and ... stupidity.

The war was illegal because it failed to be authorised by the international community – in other words, the UN. Once over, the only way to accept this situation was to get it ratified by the UN. That did not take place either. The only pseudo-legal argument in favour of the war, the presence of weapons of mass destruction, was excluded, as the US army was unable to find any. The Bush Administration told UN Inspectors that they had confidential information. That proved to be false. They had simply lied.

Actually, the whole US action was based on lies. The US lied about the weapons of mass destruction. They also lied about the reasons of the opponents of the war, who were said to be trying to recover their debts: but what are the US$1.7 billion of debts owed to France, contracted in the 1980s by Iraqis who, then at war with Iran, were buying arms with the support of the US, against the US$2.5 billion debts guaranteed by the US Exim Bank? They lied about the cheering crowds: can a mere hundred Shia dancing around a collapsed statue of Saddam Hussein be classed as a nation? Finally, they lied about the action itself. On 23 March, a Syrian bus was hit by a US missile, killing and wounding civilians. This happened "by mistake" and the US State Department even presented condolences. Yet it is now confirmed that "the shot was deliberate on the basis of information according to which Hezbollah members were in the bus" (*Le Figaro* 14/4/03). (It later transpired that they were not, and that the result had been killings of civilians instead of the targeted combatants.) In other words, as the analyst Barry put it: "The Bush Administration has falsified documents, copied university works, presented fake proofs to the UN: nobody has ever come so close to forfeiture." They lied in South East Asia, in South America, now in Iraq: duplicity is an intrinsic part of their foreign policy.

A brilliant illustration of this is when Richard Perle wrote: "The chronic incapacity of the UN Security Council to apply its own resolutions, as testified by the Iraqi case, is obvious: the organisation is simply not able to assume its mission." What about the resolutions against Israel? Why claim so often that they are not conquerors if it is so obvious. They came to install democracy and, quite contrarily, want to set up pro-American regimes with a democratic façade. Everything is being made for the sole benefit of America – to start with the companies being given reconstruction contracts without any bidding process, the payment of which is to be made from Iraqi oil resources. For years, the US did nothing against Iraq because they needed its support against the Iranian threat. After the truce between Iraq and Iran, they sustained the Kurds. Then they let them down and allowed Saddam to exterminate them. For 12 years, said Barry, "the US let Saddam Hussein make the Shia die of hunger and massacres in order to contain Teheran and please Riyadh. The US imperialist opportunists are the successors to the British colonialists, but with moralist pretensions." Such is the morale and arrogance of people, many of whom cannot even be considered representatives of the Jewish lobby but just the Likud party. Perle, Wolfowitz, Leedle and others are true representatives of those who never stood for election and who are guided by a leader who pronounced these unforgettable words: "Our mission is to fight and win the war in order to prevent us from war." This is where stupidity is not far behind.

The first mistake is to believe that a change of regime in Iraq would have a natural domino effect in the region and resolve the Palestinian problem which, according to them, would have been sorted out long ago had Syria and Iran not been backing violence. Furthermore, did they ever wonder who would win free elections if they were to be held in Syria or in Egypt? The designation of Chalabi in a first democratic move in Iraq is particularly worrying in that respect. "Installing a Pentagon crony to govern Iraq is not the same thing as building democracy," writes Stephens in the *Financial Times*. Chalabi, the man the Pentagon likes because he tells them what they want to hear, is also a person who was condemned to 22 years in jail for fraud after the US$360 million debt-ridden Jordan Petra Bank collapse. The US are never very successful with their frontmen.

A second mistake is to forget that destroying a country in the name of democracy generally leads to terrorism. Some short-sighted analysts have already claimed that pessimistic forecasts failed to materialise. Yet a historian has shown that a period of three to six months is generally witnessed between an event and an act of terrorism linked to it. There has been a sharp acceleration in Iraq; the murder of Abdul Majid Al Khoï took place just one week after the war ended. The US only rule out such a frightening development if it considers that terrorism is limited to what strikes America only. Worse, an unwelcome foreign presence in a territory will undoubtedly add local terrorism to the trans-national terrorism of Al Qaida.

A last obvious mistake is to provoke additional tension and unrest in regions that are already unstable. The same targets could probably have been achieved by means other than war. But how can this be proposed to those who wants war at any price?

To conclude, it is true to say that the direction followed by France, Germany and Russia needs to be backed by a newly strengthened Europe rather than one that limits to follow-up what others think is good for them. If British Prime Minister Tony Blair appears to some observers as the one who could help heal the war wounds between America and Europe, that does not make him "a true European". It confirms a job initiated with the help of Spain, Italy and some former eastern bloc countries, which is to consolidate American influence in Europe. Yet, if Europe's voice is to have the chance to be heard in the world, a European common foreign policy must be developed, which starts with building up a common military tool. This is the meaning of last week's meeting in Brussels: Europe is not willing to be at loggerheads with the US, nor to be the 51st State of the Union.

NEO-CONSERVATIVES DO NOT TYPIFY THE US

27 May 2003

Where is America? The question may sound odd to all those who are rightfully witnessing the implementation of Pax Americana in the region and, to start with, in Iraq: a State Department official appointed as a civil administrator, a retired American general looking after "a small business between friends", another American supervising the future oil policy of the country, an American company chosen to implement a new TV channel, not to forget the American crony Ahmed Chalabi who could not build a 20-year career as an opponent, and thus now had to do it in just a few months. As the American blueprint puts it, the next hot topic of conversation in Iraq will be free market, privatisation, electronic stock market trading and tax overhauls. The US Agency for International Development is on the verge of awarding a US$70 million contract to Bearing Point Inc. for part of the work – no bidding, of course – and other friends will join soon.

Elsewhere in the region, or indeed anywhere in the world since Richard Perle's magic words "We will not stop there; we shall continue through all means to fight against the countries who host terrorists or develop weapons of mass destruction", a "new strategic dynamic" is taking place. Syria was warned that no longer is it a question of "I put a spell on you" but more a case of "we'll keep an eye on you"; Big Brother is looking after everything – from the nine identified Palestinian organisations whose offices in Damascus should be shut down, to the Israeli–Palestinian conflict and the implementation of the roadmap. The Golan Heights was not mentioned, despite its critical importance. Secretary of State Colin Powell has just completed a tour in the region with so much apparent strength and imperial willingness that the day the US Ambassador in Israel remitted the roadmap to Ariel Sharon, another US official, Elliot Abrams, was holding private talks with him in order to assure him that he would never face any pressure from the US over it.

Indeed, hasn't the time come to start wondering whether the new giant has not become something of a paper tiger? Beyond what the *Financial Times* calls "the immediate incompetence of Rumsfeld who is making a mess of the peace", total chaos, which now seems to prevail in Iraq, is the first illustrative example. "One major conclusion one may draw from that war is that it is possible to make a totalitarian regime collapse without inflicting severe damages to a country," wrote Perle. He probably could not visit Iraq recently nor look at TV reports. Even US former Secretary of State James Baker acknowledges that "the looting was regrettable, but fully consistent with the experience of other people adjusting to the shock of liberation". That is something to say to the families whose children are blown to pieces by bombs which the US army "did not have time to collect". Baghdad has become a town where one should learn to protect oneself. Looting, theft and threats are now common practice, and disease is spreading through lack of water, as in Basra. The American army was able to isolate and demolish a weakened regime but when the country collapsed into chaos, they stood by or, worse, discarded and ignored half-perceived threats. In the meantime, Shia influence has resulted in an increase in investment in health, education, welfare and infrastructure. "US victory in the Iraq war could benefit Islamists," wrote the *Wall Street Journal*. Indeed, the Muslim Brotherhood Group is among those on the increase; was that America's plan?

Actually, the situation is hardly better elsewhere, not to mention the likely consequences of the war both economically and politically in Jordan, Egypt or Turkey and how not to react to insane comments heard from would-be analysts – actually wishful thinkers – about the false threat of possible acts of terrorism as a result of the war. Ninety people dead in Saudi Arabia last week; 30 or so in Morocco this week, and others in Israel and Occupied Palestine. Bush thought that leading the war in Iraq to make weapons of mass destruction disappear would put an end to terrorism. He was obviously wrong. Not because no weapons of mass destruction have been found to date, but simply because one does not need such a weapon to bomb a cafe. Even the World Bank chairman, Mr Wolfensohn, admits that: "One may witness that aggression, war and the lack of hope provoke a hate which can lead to terrorism." Indeed, how would any human being react to the words of an Israeli general, Israel's Defence Forces Chief of Staff Moshe Ya'alon: "The aim is to lead Palestine to internalise in the deepest recesses of their consciousness that they are a defeated people."

Here we have reference to the roadmap saga, the precise contents of which are, in fact, of limited interest, as is the emerging dialectic between those who doubt it will ever succeed (namely a growing number of Arab states) and those who will never accept it; or only with so many conditions that it is prevented from having any substance (namely the Sharon camp). The only valuable issue, actually, is to know who has the power to bring the Israelis to the negotiation table, and the answer is the US. But is this what the Bush Administration wants to do 18 months before the president runs for re-election?

When the dice are loaded, there are two ways to behave. One is to leave the game, as some Palestinian organisations immediately put it. But isn't there a bothering element for consideration: that the two clearly opposed parties to the roadmap are both Hamas and the organisations supporting Jews living in Israeli colonies built in Occupied Palestine?

Another way is to behave properly and not be reproached for anything. As long as Mahmoud Abbas avoids the risk of being cornered into a hopeless bilateral negotiation restricted to Israel and Palestine, and as long as he understands that a future for the roadmap only lies with the US and the other members of the Quartet's hands, every effort should be made to give peace a fair chance, irrespective of what the Sharon government may say, do or undo. No time is to be lost elsewhere.

A first move on the Palestinian side was to make emerge another figure who, although still representative of his people, would be better accepted by the Americans. That has been done, thanks incidentally to Yasser Arafat, who finally permitted it.

Another move could come from Syria. Because, among Arab countries, it expressed a courageous view about the US pre-emptive ideological war in Iraq, soon after the war Syria became a favourite target of the Washington neo-conservatives. The role it was playing with some Islamist terrorist groups was a major obstacle to any solution in Occupied Palestine, and crushing the Syrian regime was thus the only way to finalise the roadmap positively. Syria reacted swiftly, but it is likely that much remains to be done even though, as Henry Kissinger used to say, "Peace cannot be done without Syria." Syria stands at a geographical crossroads. For some reason, it has shelved some Palestinian extremist organisations, which also means it may have a kind of control over them, and it is smart enough to find the appropriate ways to favour the peace way to the roadmap targets within the framework of a regional settlement.

Syria understood it in the past when it began to evacuate its army from Lebanon. Continuing would be a clear signal to the international community that it is a serious partner. As the French Minister for Foreign Affairs Villepin said, "In the context of a global Middle East peace, we call on Syria to do everything possible to facilitate the application of the roadmap and Israel to accept to negotiate over a return of the Golan Heights to Syria." Irrespective of any future relationship between Lebanon and Syria, which is obviously dictated by some basic geographical considerations, the rewards could be there.

If nothing concrete materialises on the Israeli side, at least the Arab world will be able to stand proudly with the sense of duty done. It will then be up to Bush to act in accordance with his words. It is true that one may expect little from a group of people such as Richard Perle, Michael Ledeen and James Wolsey – all members of the Jewish Institute for National Security Affairs – who once declared "Our only concern is Israel." But in same way as the Likud is not Israel, the neo-conservatives are not the US. It is up to them to accept the idea that the "strategic new dynamic" is not a one-way concept, or to become, as Stephens wrote in the *Financial Times*, "A power without obvious purpose, an empire without a role."

TIES CAN'T BE BASED UPON SUBORDINATION

9 JUNE 2003

How long will it last? Role games, virtual diplomacy, false reconciliation and, last but not least, Condoleezza Rice's typical sense of humour: "Arab support is there; it goes on growing ..."

It could, indeed, only go on growing, considering where it starts from – the lowest level ever recorded among the Arab world, as a recent survey showed. Nobody would really care if, according to the same report, Osama bin Laden was rated as "the Arab leader most capable of doing the right thing regarding world affairs" by 71 per cent of people surveyed in Jordan, about the same in Egypt and 85 per cent or so in Occupied Palestine. This is one of the results of an insane war in Iraq, not because it toppled Saddam Hussein but because this could have been achieved by other means. America's difficulties in occupying Iraq and British Prime Minister Tony Blair's troubles over the alleged distortion of intelligence may only confirm the belief that there is an alternative to the American devil and the Islamic deep blue sea.

Meanwhile, US President George W. Bush goes on leading the show and, like Santa Claus, delivers good and bad marks to everyone. For instance, he began his latest European trip in Poland, the new American darling which still, however, needs big handouts from the EU budget to spend on a US exercise in Iraq; for the rest, a system based on 'divide and rule' sticks to the famous motto: "Forgive Russia, ignore Germany and punish France." Take it as it is – it is called a strategy. Virtual management of the world continued in Evian. As though in a Japanese shadow theatre, G8 members committed to work together, swore that the past was the past and avoided talking too much about the future – a pity, considering the efforts made by the host, French President Jacques Chirac, to bring in a few smaller countries such as China and Brazil, which might have had something to say. But Bush was in a hurry. As democracy in Iraq is not going to be a blockbuster, an apparently friendly picture of Bush between Israeli Prime Minister Ariel

Sharon and his Palestinian counterpart Abu Mazen would make it better. Well done; the landscape of Sharm El Sheikh is magnificent. A progression of negotiations over Palestine, which, Sharon inadvertently realised last week, was "occupied", may even help him win the next presidential race better than any unlikely implementation of a democratic civilian government soon in Baghdad. Unless, of course, having thrown the UN, the EU and Russia out of the "quartet", it all falls on his shoulders when it breaks.

Yet, as in any show, the new US diplomacy throws dust in our eyes and does not hide simple, although stunning, evidence: the Atlantic Alliance, if not dead, has been emptied out.

Some concrete signals emerged from a press growing nervous, especially those flying the banner of the neo-conservatives: in a hard-worded editorial, the *Wall Street Journal* declared war on the *Financial Times* because of a series of articles which basically said (1) that the US had decided to go to war anyway, well ahead of the UN meeting in January; (2) that Blair had knowingly exaggerated intelligence information; and (3) that the Bush Administration coordinated a divisive action in Europe, incidentally with the help of the aforementioned *Wall Street Journal*, whose Europe Editor wrote the draft of the so-called 'Letter of Eight' before it reached the desk of the Spanish prime minister. Being short of other arguments, a trash-throwing exercise started again. Well, we do not need to be shown the graves of American soldiers who died in Normandy nor remind the Poles that France declared war on Germany in 1939 for them to allow us to reflect on the following comment from the *Financial Times's* Martin Wolf: "A transatlantic alliance cannot be sustained if the US remains dedicated to its current doctrines except as a state of dependency on one side and mastery on the other." The very point, actually, is to know what we broadly want the international system to be tomorrow.

Rice, whose academic background is always referred to by the press as if it were necessary, recently answered a journalist "Multilateralism, unilateralism, unipolarity, multipolarity, what does all this mean?" In one sense she may be right, as many observers are also not sure of the distinction between "multipolarity", which would be considered as the emergence of an opposing power to the US, and "multilateralism", which would be an open-minded and more socially acceptable management tool of the international relationship. But more significantly, those who defend a "unipolar" approach know what they are doing. They, for instance, like to picture Chirac's stance in favour of a united Europe as a move against the US and another example of neo-Gaullist anti-Americanism. General de Gaulle may have had good reasons to oppose the US: the man who called for continuing the Second World War on 18 June 1940 could hardly accept that the US kept their Ambassador in Vichy until the very end, nor that they tried to set up a US-led military government over France, after preventing him from joining the June 1944 D-day Normandy landing.

But this is history. Europeans today also share common values, some of them being more common to them than to the Americans, and if internationalisation of the economy is rubbing out frontiers, still the manufacture of an Airbus aircraft creates more jobs in Europe than the manufacture of a Boeing aircraft would do. The political appreciation of a situation also may differ according to past experience or different cultural backgrounds. How do you explain otherwise, for instance, the way Europe insists that Palestinian President Yasser Arafat is not sidelined in the roadmap negotiation process? Actually, "Europe", as Philip Stephens writes in the *Financial Times*, "should coolly reassess its strategic interest, write its own security doctrine: not in opposition to the US but independent of it ... and start thinking for itself". Unilateralism, "exceptionalism" and the search for absolute security, the "neo-conservative dogma", is deeply contrary to the principles of the European integration process itself, whatever the positions of Chirac, German Chancellor Gerhard Schroeder, Spanish Prime Minister Jose Maria Aznar or Blair are on the transatlantic link. On the other hand, multipolarity means strengthening the European pole and balancing the American one, and that should be clear enough to everybody.

On the one hand, indeed, there is one super-power in both the economic and military fields. The EU as a whole is a serious economic partner or challenger, but it has not yet a military nor political power equivalent to America. So how should European countries behave with it? Limit it to establishing a bilateral relationship – something like a "fish and chips supper" with ten pounds of fish and one gram of chips? Or using what is being built together in order to be better heard? The most powerful country in the world thinks it is right to do everything alone, even by cheating – yet something Blair experienced this week in Parliament is not understood the same way on the other side of the

Atlantic. The Bush Administration considers now that its interest lies in dividing rather than unifying Europe, a total shift from previous policies, and to do that it doesn't hesitate to spend big amounts of time and money. The matter goes far beyond knowing who is eligible (or not) to be invited to George W. Bush's ranch in Texas.

The point, however, is that unrivalled power always provokes opposition, and these days the Bush Administration tends to dump into the camp of its opponents whoever does not automatically support its policies. Yet being partners doesn't necessarily mean being equal. Being different doesn't necessarily mean being enemies. But partnership cannot be based on subordination. When arrogance and sufficiency remain the two instruments of international policy, a kind of mental obesity similar to the physical one develops. It is one thing to be a super-power and another to behave as if free of any checks. What would be the state of international relationships if only the law of the strongest applies? Law is enforced to protect the weakest. International law as well. And the freedom of the weakest is to talk free; just as Shakespeare, cited by French analyst Alexis Debat, wrote in *Measure for Measure*: "O, it is excellent to have a giant's strength; but it is tyrannous to use it like a giant."

WAR OF WORDS HAS NOW BEGUN

23 JUNE 2003

War goes on in Iraq, where 50 or so American soldiers have died since US President George Bush declared that "war was over". War goes on, too, in Occupied Palestine, in Afghanistan and in so many other places in the world. Maybe one will start tomorrow in Iran, should the international community fail to stop Dr Follamour's[1] heirs, who seem to be reigning like masters on the other side of the Atlantic. "Iraq's support of terrorism was minuscule compared to Iran's activities. If we are serious about winning the war against the terror masters, the Tehran regime must fall," said Michael Ledeen[2] on 11 June. At least the message is clear. Yet another type of war has also been developing unnoticed: the "war of words".

To begin with, it appears very much like the propaganda from the good old days of the Stalinist press. Afghanistan is "freed", but the Afghan government cannot get out of Kabul without risk of its members being assassinated; Baghdad is "freed", but nobody can move alone safely on the streets despite a 150,000-strong occupation force. More surprisingly, the *Wall Street Journal* joined the game when it wrote about last week's Paris Air Show "Paris sky empty of innovations" the very day Airbus announced a US$19 billion order for new aircraft from the airline's customer Emirates. With a further order from Qatar Airways, Airbus obtained 64 orders worth US$21 billion and will, for the first time in its history, produce more planes than Boeing. But this is probably not worth a mention in some of the world's press. Yet the award will go once again to Amir Taheri writing with far-sighted judgement of the international situation in the *Wall Street Journal* and *Gulf News* (25 June): "With Saddam Hussein gone, France has no friends left in the Middle East." Arab leaders visiting Paris these days will not fail to confirm this. But why do people always feel the need to bite the hand that feeds them?

However, the new war of words is actually subtler and surely more perverse. There are examples in their hundreds. American soldiers, for instance, are not killed in Iraq because of an ambush or because the population might be dissatisfied with the occupation; they are attacked because an "organised" opposition is developing. If one goes through unrest without any major problem, possible attacks are the result of isolated or uncontrolled elements; if it becomes more difficult to go through it, then this is because an "organised" resistance is taking place. Something, according to US Defence Secretary Rumsfeld, "made of militants paid in cash by Saddam Hussein" – that same Saddam Hussein who was dead according to the same Rumsfeld when that suited him, but who has now come back to life.

Meanwhile, and as one knows, Iraq is occupied by forces of the "coalition", which are the US, the UK and Poland, which is still struggling to gather the 2000 troops required from it. The good news is that the Spanish government will "lend" it 200 soldiers, next year. This may be late, but it is still a positive move compared to Italian support. Sure, the word "canon" was used by the Italian prime minister's ally Umberto Bossi. But that was only to be used against illegal immigrants. Anyway, why should Silvio Berlusconi, the first ever European leader to visit the Middle East without meeting any Palestinian representative, stop the Italian army from joining the battlefield when the UK's Minister for Europe, Denis McShane, just forgets about him when citing the "British-Spanish-Danish-Polish" line on Iraq?

When the US is talking of implementing democracy in Iraq, do they mean they want a Shia state "legally" governed by what represents the majority of the country, with no power left to either the Sunni or the Kurds? Also do they want Sheik Yassin to be "legally" elected as a ruler of Palestine by a majority of voters? Words, after all, may sometimes be as dangerous as weapons of mass destruction. But looking fairly at a situation requires greater courage, especially when one pretends to be an arbiter. An arbiter, though, needs to be in the middle: not on one side or the other; nor, indeed, on both sides. This is something the American people should understand when the Palestinians are expressing concern about the chances of success of the roadmap process. This is a historical responsibility for the country that has become the world's super-power: acting immediately and sincerely, why not in conjunction with allies (or "former" allies as they now say), without falling into the traps of false rhetoric, biased wording and subtle (or unsubtle) propaganda. One of the main missions of those who hold power is to make people happy. To achieve this, one should act, not react.

Notes

1. Dr Follamour (Dr Strangelove) is a fictitious character in a novel by Stephen King, and a film by Stanley Kubrick. The story is of a US colonel who goes mad and decides to launch an attack on the USSR in order to save the world. The story illustrates the fact that once the process is unleashed, it becomes impossible to stop it.
2. Michael Ledeen is a former employee of the Pentagon, the State Department and the National Security Council. He is the author of *The War against the Terror Masters*.

WAR AND TERRORISM: NEVER THE TWAIN SHOULD MIX

7 JULY 2003

With every passing day, the US becomes more deeply involved in what might well be shifting Iraqi sands, with no solution likely to be found without the support of the international community. The Palestinians have agreed to a ceasefire or truce within the framework of the roadmap, which will last as long as it can. US President George W. Bush goes on declaring that his move against Iraq was "aimed at protecting the US from weapons of mass destruction", which nobody can find, as well as "continuing the fight against Al Qaida", whose link with Iraq was never proven. It looks like business as usual.

In an interesting speech by Bush, probably prepared by Condoleezza Rice, the National Security Advisor with an academic background, the American president returned to the issue of terrorism, linking the continuing war in Iraq to the broader war against Al Qaida and terrorism. He notably declared that: "These groups who believed they have shaken our resolve in the War on Terror or caused us to leave Iraq before freedom is fully established, were wrong and would not succeed." If Bush had declared that, since 11 September 2001, military power no longer ensures the total security of a nation, he would have made a step forward. But like a diplomacy that has a long track record of missing elements, Bush continues to carry forward some misunderstandings that may cost him a re-election.

The point is, his use of the word "terrorism" should not be accepted any more, not least because it leads nowhere. "Our problem is Hamas," declared White House spokesman Ariel Fleisher, which makes as much sense as saying "Our problem is terrorism". Actually, our problem is what keeps terrorism alive; what makes Hamas and other movements develop. Pope John Paul II recently declared that: "Looking for the deep roots of terrorism is a compulsory task for whoever wishes to fight against this phenomenon." Let's start providing decent living conditions to people living in refugee camps; let's start teaching children; let's start leaving peasants alone to cultivate their fields; and let's stop feeding ourselves with inappropriate general concepts that were designed for other environments.

But one should then move on another step and think about who is actually a terrorist and who is not. When a country publicly admits that it conceived and has put into action an official policy of political assassinations, how can it argue that it should not occupy equal billing with "terrorist" groups? When one assumes that killing an Israeli illegal coloniser is an "act of terrorism", but firing a rocket from a helicopter to get rid of a political leader, and eventually killing his wife and daughter, is an "act of war", it is pretty clear that caution should prevail when defining words. In so many aspects, war, and what some people call terrorism (especially in the Middle East), are just two different sides of the same ugly face of violence. War may be legal or illegal, the same as terrorism, which, very often, becomes "legal" once it seizes power: were not Ben Gurion and Golda Meir "Zionist terrorists" in the eyes of the British colonial troops in the 1930s? When Israeli Prime Minister Ariel Sharon decided to assassinate Dr Abdulaziz Al Rantissi to ensure that Hamas would react using the well-known scenario of suicide attacks followed by other retaliations, isn't his action just the same as that of those he condemns? Once again, one should not confuse terrorism and national liberation movements. This is why the words of General de Gaulle again come to mind: "Israel organises on territories it conquered; an occupation which cannot go on without oppression, repression and expulsion. And a form of resistance develops against it, which it calls terrorism."

Finally, attention should also be given to the form to be taken by violence. Isn't an illegal occupation of a territory for several years a terrible and continuing form of violence? Isn't the presence of 500 illegal Jewish colonisers protected by 1000 Israeli soldiers in the midst of an Arab city of 120,000 a fact of continuing violence? Isn't a forthcoming fence, a kind of self-indicted ghetto belt, an unbearable violence? Nassi Hifti, the Arab League Ambassador to France, recently summed up the Israeli violence as follows: "I provoke you in order to create violence, and to comfort me in my immobilism which in turn, creates violence."

The ongoing story of people seeking their nation's independence will not stop in Occupied Palestine. Interestingly enough, some illegal Jewish settlers recently argued that "nobody has required the Americans to give their land back to the Indians". Maybe they agreed with the Arab poet Adonis, who told us of the running bird who "witnesses the resurrection of the Indian of America in Palestine ..."

The time has now come to call a war a war, and to stop confusing ourselves with words such as "war" or "terrorism", which seem to apply differently to different situations but actually have similar effects. What is at stake is the use or non-use of violence, and that is a complex issue with no clear-cut answer. For the time being, nobody could have concluded better than Palestinian Prime Minister Mahmoud Abbas addressing Ariel Sharon last week: "Our conflict with you is a political conflict and we will end it through political means."

SPEAKING THE TRUTH HELPS TO BUILD MUTUAL UNDERSTANDING

20 JULY 2003

The war in Iraq was illegal. This may be nothing new to *Gulf News* readers, but surely it is to readers of the British press.

> The case that needed proving to justify war was that it presented a current and serious threat. The intelligence to make this case is now discredited – and with it the *casus belli* ... Neither (presented) argument is a legitimate reason for invading a sovereign country and toppling its government.

So wrote the influential *Financial Times* in a recent issue at a time when the pressure on British Prime Minister Tony Blair is reaching unforeseen proportions. In the beginning, there was an immediate threat represented by weapons of mass destruction which, according to Blair, "were actionable in 45 minutes". When it appeared that these arms could not be found, a first signal appeared in the *Wall Street Journal* under the form of an article urging that "all necessary efforts" be made to find them. But that ran short too, and supporters of the war said that, actually, there were other reasons for toppling the regime, such as liberating the Iraqi people and, through Saddam Hussein's removal, eliminating a threat to regional stability. "The war has seen a serial international criminal removed, a known threat eliminated, a butcher of his own people deposed," wrote Gerard Baker of the Hoover Institute. But there are so many butchers on earth, and the *Financial Times* concludes bluntly: "Pre-emptive action has no support in international law unless there is a serious and immediate threat. This was lacking."

The only thing we now have to do is wait for Condoleezza Rice, who has an academic background, to explain to us the difference between a lie and an error of interpretation; and for Blair to remind us of the virtues of "working together", probably not, however, with the Italian secret services who have recently proved yet again their lack of efficiency.

In the meantime, the US army will continue to suffer daily casualties and beg additional military support from other members of the "alliance". It seems that only Israeli Prime Minister Ariel Sharon's close friend and Italian counterpart, Silvio Berlusconi, is prepared to send the Italian army to Iraq. The point is, nobody asked him. "If one has a hammer, everything looks like a nail. What is happening in Iraq is a telling indication of these limits," writes Martin Wolf in the *Financial Times*. The cost of these limits is $1 billion per week.

In this regard, there are figures that deserve to be compared.

> Between November 2000 and December 2002, the EU granted nearly €250 million to keep the Palestinian administration alive and to sustain the most basic of public services ... We cannot expect peace to take roots unless ordinary people see the benefits of change and gain confidence that improved conditions are here to stay.

This statement was recently made by European Commissioner Christopher Pattern. This is where Europe stands. The contrary view is: "The refugees seem like an insurmountable problem only because the Arab leaders are intent on keeping them as one." This is what the Bush Administration's supporter, *Wall Street Journal*, writes. We are not setting Europe against the US, but calling a cat a cat.

Incidentally, one should also thank Sharon, who was expressing himself recently about illegal Jewish colonies being dismantled in front of TV cameras, then re-occupied a few hours later: "It is allowed to establish settlements in the colonies, but it is needless to talk about it, nor to organise a party every time a construction permit is granted." Speaking the truth helps in understanding. Especially if one succeeds in creating a friendly environment as a first step towards mutual confidence-building. "Abbas should remember that until he produces real results on the ground, he only commands international favour because he is not Arafat," writes the *Wall Street Journal* about Abu Mazen, "a relatively weak man who has a tendency to escape the problems", according to the US Ambassador in Tel Aviv, Dan Kurtzer. With such friends, who needs enemies?

However, one should not waste time watching the Anglo-Saxon camp settle its internal conflicts, and attention is better focused on what is of most important essence – for instance, a recent statement by Gerald Steinberg, Director of the Programme on Conflict Management and Negotiation at the Bar Ilan University:

> The public has little faith in unfulfilled promises; it wants an immediate divorce, based on the unilateral construction of the reparation fence ... When complete, the combination of a concrete wall, trenches, electronic sensors and patrol roads is expected seriously to impede terrorist access to Israelis cities.

At a time when people of good faith are discussing how to reach peace, others are building a wall which, officially, will protect Israeli cities from terrorism. But this is not true – not only because it doesn't work, as some activist groups recently proved, but because living on earth means living together. From its very origins, humankind has been learning how to live together, how to ensure that one side doesn't eliminate another. This has not gone smoothly, as wars or massacres may testify. But the move was unabated in spite of its ups and downs, and if ghettos or apartheid policies have not all disappeared, at least the direction was clear. It is not for half of a population to live on one side of the fence and for the other half to live on the other side. But the erection of the wall – an unbelievable act of continuing violence – answers other Israeli demands: enlarging already occupied lands, protecting illegal colonies, anticipating future borders irrespective of any ongoing discussions, and fixing them in concrete and tears.

Some of the ugliest pages of history have been marked down by the concept of the ghetto, but a ghetto in those times was directly or indirectly imposed by the strongest on the weakest. It is now the other way round: they are inflicting on themselves their own ghetto behind their wall. Yet Sharon should remember, those who erected walls, including replicas of the "wall of shame", historically proved always to be wrong.

THE SEVEN MORTAL SINS OF AMERICAN BLINDNESS

5 AUGUST 2003

A few months ago, opponents of the war in Iraq used to say that whatever action the Bush Administration would take unilaterally, it would need the rest of the world to win the peace. Although the number of daily casualties in the American army confirms such predictions, US President George W. Bush and his Defence Secretary Donald Rumsfeld stick to their previous position, at least officially, and seem to be fully satisfied with their status as an occupying power. "For sure," writes the *Wall Street Journal*, "550,000 NATO compliant troops would be fine, but not at the cost of giving them [France and Germany] or the UN substantial say over the future of Iraq." They will thus continue with their coalition of "more than 30 countries over eight time zones", which is basically a few soldiers from here and there to be commanded by a Polish army hard pressed to provide the required number of troops. They will pay for everything or reimburse all costs. Yet American law does not permit direct payment of foreign soldiers. This false internationalisation will not fool anybody and "even if there are good weeks", they can't rebuild Iraq on their own. Not recognising this is their first sin.

A second major sin against a clever vision of Iraq's future is to believe that they will be able to build a new Iraq, not only alone but in their own image. In today's Iraq, the occupying American troops think American, work American and fly the American banner every instant. From the creation of a 7000-strong civilian troop to the implementation of a police academy – a school for judges or teachers – America feels at home in Iraq. Western free market-style economic rules are being introduced, an Iraq trade bank being shaped, supply contracts being provided by a company called Halliburton whose quarterly results were never so good for years – all facts that, logically, should have a negative impact on those who do not share the same vision. And there may be many of them. The point, however, is that the US has put in place leaders they like rather than those the Iraqis want. Sooner or later, there can only be a reaction to that.

One step further towards misunderstanding is taken when arrogant behaviour prevents any kind of fair analysis. For example, it may be more convenient for the US army to describe the ongoing guerrilla war as a military unrest favoured by former Baathist partisans. But it is likely wrong, as confirmed by crucial information recently collected by experts. Bypassing Iraqi national sentiment may lead to significant mistakes of appreciation, and that third sin can hardly be forgiven.

Yet that's still minute when one thinks about what happened to the American capacity to treat intelligence material. In a self-convincing exercise, the *Wall Street Journal* editor (whose justifying comments about the war in Iraq, "We did it because we had to do it", have now been immortalised) recently summed up the situation in Occupied Palestine as follows: "Middle East Peace Progress: Israelis are releasing prisoners; Palestinian groups have been coerced into at least a temporary ceasefire." How was this success achieved? "Because Bush has taken time to de-legitimise Arafat" and in Iraq "to remove the most significant threat to Israel's existence". The truth, actually, is that Israeli Prime Minister Ariel Sharon was able to drag Bush into the trap of the fight against terrorism, preventing him from pointing out the numerous obligations ignored by the Israelis in their own commitment towards the roadmap. It looked like another of Bush's weaknesses, as illustrated by the appalling comment after last week's meeting with Sharon about the wall of shame: words to the effect of, "I do not like it, but what can I do since you do not want to stop it?" He added, "Anyway, I hope it will become irrelevant." That was a venal sin; but not resisting the Israeli approach of putting a veil on their own atrocities and shining light on the fight against terrorism is a more serious capital sin. And the list is not over!

The next three sins have a European flavour. The first one consists of continuing to divide Europe. To do that, an old recipe suggests trying to separate France and Germany on the one hand, and to insult France on the other. As far as insults are concerned, it is true to say that although probably not progress for humanity, UK tabloids have now been overtaken by US newspapers such as the *Wall Street Journal*: "With Saddam Hussein gone, France has no friends left in the Middle East", "Mahatir, the new friend of Chirac", or "France interest in Iraq barely extended beyond oil and arms contracts", etc. This is actually of no value and could even prove useful to *Wall Street Journal's* readers who will now learn that there is something to the west and east of America. Dividing France and Germany may appear to be more simple, provided it is done smartly. When quoting the German Foreign Affairs Minister, who said "Transatlantic relations are a cornerstone of freedom and stability in the 21st century", one should not miss out the rest of the statement: "The strongest country alone is not strong enough."

The sixth sin is more serious because it has historical roots which may look as though they have a continuing effect. We come back to the old accusations of the Gaullist aspirations of "glory" and the vision of a Europe which Chirac would dream of leading through forming a Western alliance and setting up a multilateral world in which Europe rivals the US. This transatlantic rivalry is nothing new – at least in the commercial, agricultural, industrial and cultural fields. The point is to show how much an "arrogant" France would like to "lead the world" against the US. Sad to say, hate doesn't favour keen analysis.

That is the final sin which cannot be forgiven: the US have not yet understood what happened in Europe over a period of many years. Did they ever realise the strength of support enjoyed by Chirac and German Chancellor Gerhard Schroeder from not only German and French but also Spanish, Italian and even British public opinion? Yet the time is no more for France to "lead" its European partners. The old Europe was that of nationalism; the new one is an integrated Europe and, as the *Financial Times* concludes: "We should thank the US for that."

EUROPE VERSUS AMERICA?

17 August 2003

America's new foreign policy, which is notably based on a unilateral appreciation of the need for pre-emptive actions, tends to divide Europe into two parts: one made of countries favouring a strong western alliance under the helm of America and those dreaming of a multipolar world, even at the expense of seeing "Europe becoming a rival to the US". Good and bad marks are then distributed in consequence: for the "willing", all members of the "new Europe", an invitation to a ranch in Texas; for the "unwilling", traditionally good but turned-out-to-be-bad friends of America and all members of the "old Europe", insults and threats. Such "analysis", despite its intellectually frightening aspect, is not only basic; it is wrong.

To start with, it seems that any political or economic relationship between Europe and America never looked like a strong alliance. Actually, it has been a story of rivalry for at least 150 years. "The struggle for supremacy has been a feature of US–European relations since America emerged as a great power in the late 19th century," writes Christopher Layne of the Washington Cato Institute. Fierce opposition in cultural, agricultural or industrial fields is blatant these days. In spite of the fantastic competitive edge of the American economy, European companies have progressed in a way that may now put them on an equal footing, as witnessed by Airbus in aeronautics, Aventis in pharmaceuticals and Nokia in mobile telephony. Many others are set to join these companies in the future, as this move is not going to slow down. A reflection of fair competition in an open liberal market, this rivalry should be "organised and not destructive" as in the words of analyst Alexandre Adler: both Europe and America need each other, and need to trade and exchange. But it seems that this situation is felt as a threat by the US to their hegemony; that they are no more ready to accept it now than they were after the First and Second World Wars. Citing former Secretary of State Dean Acheson, who wanted to preclude Europe from "becoming a third force or opposing force", Layne concludes that the so-called western alliance is only acceptable to the US provided it is US-dominated; any support to an integrated Europe is "conditional on its taking place within the framework of a US-dominated Atlantic community". Europe is authorised to exist as long as it behaves along the lines decided by America.

Playing a game of divide, taking any occasion to undermine "the European sense of common purpose", the US Administration showed at which point it was easy for it on the occasion of the war in Iraq to drag the weakest behind it, to mount the ones against the others, to trigger memories of old European quarrels and to show an arrogance which is often the first sign of a declining hegemony. Because this is also increasingly in evidence: since 11 September 2001, America has been frightened. Its leadership is no longer what it used to be 30 years earlier. The Bush Administration may have given the feeling that American hegemony was an "unchallengeable fact of international life", but this was resisted as was any imperial hegemony, history shows, whenever it occurred. Therefore, once this rivalry and the existence of an American super-power which has fought for its supremacy over the last 100 years is admitted, but whose future hegemony may be at stake, what should Europe do?

European debate, especially in France, has lacked for years the lustre that such important matters normally deserve. However, this is now changing all over Europe, and the war in Iraq surely has some responsibility. (Have not, incidentally, the US ever drawn any conclusions from the European public support enjoyed by Chirac and Schroeder during the Iraqi war?) A first step for Europe is to take stock of its situation and list the tools it can use to achieve its project, which is obviously not limited to searching for weapons of mass destruction nor fighting against terrorism: this is of particular importance when any Palestinian fighter is a "terrorist" for a Bush Administration which meanwhile does not hesitate to enter into scandalous deals with Colonel Gaddafi of Libya.

Europe actually enjoys a lot of trumps: a common constitution, fundamental treaties and a positive law which applies in a growing manner to all the member states; working institutions with 50 years of experience and a forthcoming Intergovernmental Conference which will ratify new voting rules and result in a Commission President elected by a Parliament benefiting from a €100 billion budget, 20,000 civil servants and representing 450 millions habitants. One field for further integration, military co-operation, unfortunately still lags behind. Despite initial success for a better European-integrated defence industry, member states' limited national budgets for defence policies have not yet allowed for creating this much-needed European defence capacity, which will ultimately make NATO useless. It is indeed a clear trend that, sooner or later, NATO will disappear as the military future of Europe goes through the implementation of an autonomous European security and defence policy, the only road to be followed by those who wish to get some respect from America. Developments that took place in Brussels a few months ago are thus moving in the right direction, as the American outburst about it would confirm, but there is still a long road ahead.

A second step for Europe is to make sure that, as with any club, whoever wants to join it is prepared to abide by its rules. The UK and new eastern entrants obviously spring to mind. In respect of the UK, this is nothing new as Philip Stephens reminds us in the *Financial Times*: "This administration is, like its predecessors, unwilling to defy Britain's geography to take it from the margins to the heart of Europe." In opposition to France, which feared the US would always try to impose their views on Europe, Britain thought that the only way to be important in the world was to exert influence from inside, even though the price for it is alignment. More recently, some analysts argued in the *Financial Times* that: "Only a club of three can bring European unity." This is presently obvious in the defence field, as nobody sees how Europe could be militarily integrated without the UK, France and Germany working together. But is this the true question? On the other hand, it needs to be considered whether members of a club enjoy being together and share common values. There is no compulsory joining, but Europe is not a teller machine which one may use when it fits or when it is needed. Actually, a very current issue is that there is no reason why a reinforced co-operation in the military field between states willing to move ahead together would not be possible. Who would blame the Lithuanian army Chief of Staff (incidentally a former colonel in the US army) to feel as European as a close military ally of the US? Yet it does not give him the right to prevent members of a club it is just about to join moving further ahead together and joining forces – especially when time is running short, because those who are hegemonic today may not be tomorrow. Europe's obligation is thus to organise and strengthen itself better and quicker so that the 17th-century poet John Donne's words don't apply to it: "No man is an island ... And therefore never send to know for whom the bell tolls; it tolls for Thee."

NO SUPER-POWER, HOWEVER MIGHTY, RULES THE WORLD ALONE

1 September 2003

The bombing of the UN building in Baghdad on 19 August and the suicide attack the same day in Occupied Jerusalem are two dramatic events which may look unconnected. While the first event is further dramatic proof of the occupying US army's inability to restore law and order in Iraq, the second proves that terrorism is just another ugly face of a violence that can also be 'continued', as the Israeli government shows every day in Palestine through illegal colonisation and the construction of the wall.

Yet, the US President George W. Bush claims these two events are connected:

> Iraq constitutes today a pivotal axis of the global war against terrorism. Our soldiers are fighting against terrorists in Iraq, in Afghanistan and elsewhere so that our citizens do not suffer terrorist violence in New York, St Louis or Los Angeles. As long as the Palestinians do not act seriously against terrorism, there can be no progress in the diplomatic arena.

A link might, therefore, exist between the two events, but surely not for the reasons put forward by Bush. Both events, in Baghdad and Occupied Jerusalem, actually prove that any super-power, however powerful it may be, cannot manage the world alone.

In Iraq, the situation deteriorates daily. "The occupying power is responsible for implementing law, order and security. We had hoped that coalition forces would by now have succeeded in making the environment safe enough to allow us [the UN] to lead our reconstruction mission with success. This did not happen," said UN General Secretary Kofi Annan. Nobody knows how long it will take and how many people, including American and other soldiers, will have to die before the two following elements are seriously and finally taken into consideration by the Bush Administration.

The first one relates to the UN. In an organised world, the UN cannot forever be held to the sole role of providing humanitarian assistance. One is reminded of what French Foreign Minister Dominique de Villepin said some weeks ago: "Our conviction from the very beginning is that the solution is political before it is military. It is of essence to encourage quickly the return to the plain sovereignty of Iraq and that this transition be placed under the responsibility of the UN." However, even though Anglo-Saxon observers also seem to be shifting position, this is not yet the talk of the day. "The matter consisting of conceding authority doesn't belong to the questions which we discussed," said the US Secretary of State Colin Powell after a meeting with Annan. But the Bush Administration may not be able to hold to this position very much longer. "Mr Bush's foreign policy has been based primarily on freeing the US from multilateral constraints; his guiding assumption is if the US leads forcefully enough, others will follow. To cede any meaningful control to the UN now would allow Bush's Democratic rivals at home and his critics abroad to argue that his approach was misguided," said a writer in the *Financial Times*, although in a face-saving exercise, Bush could embrace an internationalisation strategy enhancing his chances of success and minimising present costs.

The other element is that only self-rule will bring stability to Iraq. "Transitional administrations can succeed only if they allow responsibility to be taken over quickly by credible representative figures from among the population," said Edward Mortimer, the Director of Communication in Annan's office. How, indeed, can Iraqis accept that money from the sale of their oil is paid into a bank account which only Paul Bremer[1] can operate? How can they accept that an Israeli archaeological mission may now be working in Babylon closely guarded by the US army? There is a need for transfer of responsibilities that allows the Iraqis fully to assume their duties, through the implementation of an elected assembly which will choose a provisionary government and work at a new constitution. "It is time to move ahead towards a logic of sovereignty for Iraq," said Villepin, and it is clear that this also goes for the implementation of an international force acting under a new UN mandate to be voted for. Otherwise, there may be more than the usual terrorist threats mentioned by Bush. "The removal of Saddam Hussein is an integral part of winning the war against terror," he said in July [2003]. But "repeating an argument is not making a case for it; the prospect of more wars like Iraq may justify a larger defence budget for the US army but the war on terrorism does not," echoed William A. Niskanen, Chairman of the Cato Institute. Or, according to Professor Jessica Stern, a former aide of President Clinton as Director for Russian, Ukranian and Eurasian Affairs at the National Security Council: "America transformed into a terrorist threat a country which was not." There is a risk the region may become even more fragile, especially if and when the Shias decide to join what is today a non-coordinated mix of Baathist loyalists, Sunni nationalists, tribal groups, criminal elements and Islamist militants from all over the world. Then America may again leave, as it did from Beirut after 241 US servicemen were killed by a bomb blast. That was just 20 years ago.

In Palestine, the roadmap was supposed to be a multilateral approach co-ordinated by the US, UN, EU and Russia. It turned out to be a US-led exercise in Israeli defence. The role of an impartial arbiter, which the US wanted to play, disappeared with the arrival of the neo-conservatives and other "Zionist protestants" in Washington. A blatant example is the way Israelis have so far succeeded in making the issue violence-related. But "fighting against terrorism will not solve anything", as French President Jacques Chirac said, "... because in order to fight against terrorism ... one has to fight against the diseases, such as unresolved local conflicts, which extremist ideologies feed themselves with". In the specific case of Palestine, nobody knows how many people will have to die before the Bush Administration accepts such basic points: a full implication of the Quartet[2] members; a non-discriminatory approach towards any interlocutor, including elected President Yasser Arafat; an effective dismantling of illegal Jewish colonies; an immediate halt to the construction of the wall; a release of prisoners and un-blocking of cities; effective means given to the Palestinian authority to ensure law and order. Speculating about internal dissension within Hamas or between Arafat and Palestinian Prime Minister Mahmoud Abbas is, in some ways, an internal Palestinian affair. But "speculating over the steps of a roadmap which doesn't foresee any coercive mechanism towards one or the other of the parties", as writes analyst Denis Duclos, Research Director with CNRS (French National Centre for Scientific Research), "is like offering to the most powerful of the two indefinite fields of waiting". And time is running short. Should the diabolic spiral of suicide attacks/targeted assassinations not stop, there will be no choice other than the presence of an international pacifying force on the ground.

The alternative is quite simple: terrorism will obviously explode and in a few years time, demography will be the decider: 3.3 million Palestinians today versus 6.4 million Israelis; 7.4 and 9 million respectively in 25 years time according to UN statistics. Aren't Israelis smart enough to understand, like the Afrikaners, that sooner or later similar causes produce the same effects?

Notes

1. Ambassador L. Paul Bremer III was named Presidential Envoy to Iraq on 6 May 2003 and was the Administrator of the Coalition Provisional Authority in Iraq until the transfer of power in July 2005. During his 23-year State Department career, Ambassador Bremer served as Special Assistant or Executive Assistant to six Secretaries of State. His overseas assignments have included service at many embassies abroad. He also served as Executive Secretary of the State Department and was President Reagan's Ambassador at Large for Counter Terrorism. Ambassador Bremer is considered as one of the world's leading experts on crisis management, terrorism and homeland security. Yet, his record in Iraq has been put into question with regard to two main issues: the advisability of the dismantling of the Iraqi army, and the management of significant amounts of money deriving from the proceeds of Iraqi oil sales.
2. The US, the EU, the UN and Russia formed a group known as the "Quartet" which worked on the composition of a common document proposing solutions for the resolution of the Israeli–Palestinian conflict. The Quartet issued a statement regarding a "roadmap for peace" on 17 September 2002; other more detailed versions were published afterwards. The plan was largely accepted by the Palestinians and the Israelis, but with many reservations. Today, the plan has still not been implemented, notably due to the absence of objective criteria allowing for a fair evaluation of each of the various steps in the document. Furthermore, the roadmap calls for a progressive approach, whereby difficulties are settled one after the other. This requires a climate of mutual confidence that now seems to have disappeared between the two parties.

US'S MISGUIDED FOREIGN POLICIES EXPOSE
ITS POLITICAL JUVENILITY

15 September 2003

Americans are said to have little knowledge of geography. But is it up to the point of confusing the Iraqi and Palestinian battlefields? One may indeed believe that a 150,000-strong force would probably be better utilised these days on the Palestinian–Israeli border than anywhere else in the world, including Iraq.

In Iraq, the situation is developing as anticipated. The "I told you so" behaviour is of limited value, especially when people are dying every day. However, there's nothing wrong with anticipating the truth: neither America nor any other country in the world can make it alone. The conservative US press continues to insult France in a move probably aimed at asking for its help. Many observers are now making more mistakes. The first one consists of focusing the discussion on secondary issues: "Who should lead the occupation forces?", "Should the US army share its power?", "Which place should be left to the UN?", and so on. The second one is to tell France something like: "You may have been right, but the past is the past so let's now work at the future together; don't fail to realise it is also in your interest to be heard again in the US and elsewhere." Such comments show that, at the end of the day, the Bush Administration still does not understand what is at stake.

In Iraq, Americans have simply lost their way and the only thing to do is try the other way round; not a slight shift of direction but a complete u-turn. They must accept the fact that what they thought was a military issue is actually a political one. This is a complete change of logic and an additional military presence on the ground will obviously change nothing in the prevailing dramatic situation. Recently, French Foreign Minister Dominique de Villepin said:

> One should shift from a logic of occupation into a logic of development under the responsibility of the Iraqis themselves; it is politically necessary to give sovereignty back to Iraq and transfer executive

power to its institutions. The conviction of France is that one should immediately proceed to the devolution of the political power to the Iraqis.

It is irrelevant whether the Ukrainians should be commanded by Polish or British army officers. If there is a need for a multinational force, this should be put under the orders of the new Iraqi authorities. Even US President George W. Bush's supporters are changing their minds. Some, such as William Kristol, are criticising Secretary of Defence Donald Rumsfeld for bungling the after-war planning. "Put the Iraqis in charge!" writes Bernard Lewis in the *Wall Street Journal*, concluding: "If this is how it all works out, the inevitable UN wrangling may well be worth it." Just a few days earlier, the Journal was still sticking to Deputy Defence Secretary Paul Wolfowitz's view that "there is no sovereignty without security". But there is also no sovereignty without freely elected leaders and the sooner the better. Today there is no sovereignty in Iraq. Each of the 25 ministries is supervised by an American advisor and all ministers have to report to the members of the Provisory Government Council, whose members were themselves appointed by the American occupying army.

Yet another mistake is to believe that American democracy can be easily exported. The principle of "one man one vote" may have terrible effects in a country where ethnic or religious groups are so different from each other. For instance, do the Americans wish that in the future the legally elected rulers of the country all come from the Shia community, which make up two-thirds of the population? As the analyst Denis Lacorne put it: "Real democracy remains to be built and it will not be easy: a complex system of weighted votes, protected minorities, reshaped territories, a system which maybe only exists in Switzerland!" Olivier Roy, a Research Director at CNRS, adds: "It is terrible to see the no-exit situation in which the Americans stand today because they believed Iraq was like Nazi Germany and they were going to reconstruct like in 1945." Political space should be reopened to give sovereignty back to the Iraqis and let them decide what is good for them.

This is far removed from Anglo-Saxon calls to France "to back President Bush's new resolution at the UN" as it is. The actual question is not that the role of the UN should be enlarged; it is to make precise the role of the UN. As former Lebanese minister Ghassan Salamé recently said: "One should launch a political process aiming at involving the

Iraqis in the defence of their institutions." This can happen through a re-building of the Iraqi power, replacing foreign occupying forces by Iraqi forces, reintegration of all the excluded components of the Iraqi society who have no other choice today than plotting against the state, and the setting-up of a public and precise calendar with strict timetables in a reasonably short period of time. Going back to the UN with no intention of changing the contents of the foreign presence in Iraq is perfectly useless, whatever the position of France, Germany, Russia and others. No international settlement can take place with unilateralism, especially when this strategy derives from a country that sometimes seems to have no leader. Besides the controversial aspects of Bush's election, a country which is daily ridiculed by the Sharon government and which is unable to arbitrate between its State Department and the Pentagon, can only give room to stories such as the latest one about the way in which the Mujahideen-e-Khalq issue was handled.[1] When one reads that a reason for the US to go to the UN is to obtain a kind of validation of what has happened in order to secure the conditions which will allow countries such as Turkey, India or Pakistan to send troops, just because "Muslim soldiers would better be accepted by the Iraqi population", it is clear that the Bush Administration has not yet realised where and how it has gone wrong. "Washington seems only to want cash and troops for what Bush called the central front in the war against terrorism. But signing up to a failed policy will only deepen and multiply its consequences." This was written in the *Financial Times* last week. How many people will have to die before we read that in an American newspaper? World security cannot be protected without hearts being won.

NOTES

1 The Mujahideen-e-Khalq (MeK) organisation is the largest Iranian opposition group. It was founded in the mid-1960s by a group of people mixing Marxist and Islamic principles. It fought an armed struggle in the early 1970s against the Shah of Iran and was accused of conducting several assassinations of US military personnel based in Iran. The organisation helped Ayatollah Ruhollah Khomeini to seize power in Tehran in 1979 and to set up his administration (it was also present at the US Embassy during the hostage crisis of 1979), but soon came under attack for its secularist ideology. It was driven out of Iran and resettled in Paris. The organisation supported Iraq during the 1981–8 war and established a military wing in 1987, called the "National Liberation Army" which occasionally teamed-up with the Iraqi army. It was declared a "Foreign Terrorist Organisation" by the US in 1997, which did not prevent the Bush Administration from striking a deal with them in early 2003 on the occasion of the war in Iraq. The organisation is said to benefit from a 20,000-strong guerrilla force. Its President-in-exile is Mrs Maryam Rajavi whose husband Massoud Rajavi leads the "National Council of Resistance of Iran".

TIME TO OFFER SHARON A ONE-WAY TICKET

29 SEPTEMBER 2003

To kill or not to kill Arafat? That should have never been the question – simply because in a democracy, one does not raise the types of issues that are normally left to Mafia gatherings. However, after yet another arrogant speech by US President George W. Bush at the UN, observers are commenting on the new American foreign policy – "Talk to the Germans, buy the Russians and isolate the French" – that it is necessary to return to this matter one month after the facts, if only because they took place during an Israeli government cabinet meeting in a country that claims to be "the only democracy in the Middle East". Wondering whether it is better to kill the legal representative of the Palestinian people doesn't seem to have raised any particular moral issue. Israeli lobbies justified it through the US press by Hamas's behaviour. When one starts using the same means as the condemned, terror is not far away and everybody knows where "no liberty for the enemies of liberty" leads. This was also a reason why former Israeli Prime Minister Menachem Begin used to say that it would be impossible in the long run for the Israeli democracy to settle the Palestinian conflict only through the use of force. The current Prime Minister Ariel Sharon has made a big leap forward since then.

Despite a fantastic wave of protest throughout the world, the Bush Administration limited itself to saying that "it was not a good idea", not an "efficient way to behave" and finally, "a way to put Arafat back on track". A resolution at the UN Security Council demanding that "Israel desist from any act of deportation and cease any threat to the safety of the elected president of the Palestinian Authority" was vetoed by the US in a clear indication that they are turning their back on the peace process. The resolution was ultimately voted for by 133 countries at the General Assembly. But everyone knows that only resolutions pertaining to Iraq are taken into account by the Bush Administration. A reason for vetoing the resolution was that it failed "to condemn the Palestinian terrorism".

That should have been a reason to abstain from voting in the proposed resolution rather than vetoing it. Yet when one comes to Israel, Americans are tight-handed. As former Israeli Prime Minister Benjamin Netanyahu once said: "I don't mind what the Americans think; I have a majority in Congress."

The present alignment of the Bush Administration on the Israeli policy led by Sharon has been a noteworthy element of US foreign policy in the last two years. As long as the impact was limited to Sharon ridiculing the US, it was of little importance. "The wall creates a problem," Bush said, but Sharon didn't care what went on since he knew there would be no reaction or retaliation to maintaining and developing illegal Jewish colonies in Occupied Palestine, continuing targeted assassinations and all the other usual stuff. Yet leading a war in Iraq was a more serious affair, as it now appears that Iraq was not invaded because of September 11 but because it represented a threat to Israel. The invasion had actually been planned a long time ago, as research shows, by people whom Bush took in his luggage to the White House and the so-called fundamentalist Christians or Zionist protestants, commonly identified with the neo-conservatives, who today make American foreign policy. The point is that it is very similar to Israeli foreign policy, as strikingly evidenced by their communication channels, including the opinion pages of the *Wall Street Journal*. In a worrying trend and on a step-by-step basis, information is progressively travestied so that it can match the underlying opinions: "Britons can thank Mr Blair," the Journal wrote last week, a few days before the Labour party suffered an electoral disaster in the Brent East by-election when it lost a seat to the Liberal Democrats; "Iraq is progressing," it said, quoting Colin Powell who had just come back from Iraq where, the independent press reported, he was under heavy guard and cut off from the population. Who, then, will be surprised when Bush declares that "no link between Al Qaida and Saddam's regime was proven", even though 67 per cent of the American population still believe it's the other way round?

With Israel presently standing on both sides of the fence, it is becoming increasingly difficult for America to play a role in the Middle East conflict. Whereas it seems that the roadmap peace process will soon end (only US National Security Advisor Condoleezza Rice recently said that "it remained a valuable guide of the vision of President Bush", which is comforting in our view), any other plan to be imposed on both parties will require a strong impartial arbiter. Indeed, the Likud party is pressing for a network of fences that will connect Jewish colonies to Israel by restricted bypass roadways, penning the Palestinian population into several cantons where it may enjoy self-government but not sovereignty – a new version of the US Indian reserves and an old version of apartheid. Palestinians are in favour of one single state with voting rights. Demography shows that Palestinians will outnumber Israelis and dissolve the Jewish state. This is why the question is not whether one should or should not kill Arafat. The answer is that Sharon and the neo-conservatives should leave if one wants to progress towards a fair peace. Since he took power in February 2001, Sharon's record is a mixture of failures and intellectual perversions: from maintaining the confusion in the differences between terrorism and national liberation movements so as to suggest they are in fact the same reality, to the diabolic ability he exerted in transforming any political matter into an all-security related issue. Indicted for the Shabria and Shatilla massacres, Sharon jeopardised the roadmap in so many ways that nobody can take him seriously any more. Attacks doubled during his reign and his fascist-type policy has claimed more and more innocent victims. Israel is not Sharon. Three years after his utterly provocative visit to the Dome of the Rock Mosque in Jerusalem, it is time to offer Mr Sharon a one-way ticket.

EUROPE'S CHOICE: TO BE A POWER OR REMAIN A VASSAL

13 OCTOBER 2003

Some days are like that: when nothing can prevent the horizon from darkening further. The re-launching of the roadmap process a few months ago [in May 2003] produced so few new expectations, which are already vanishing. A fresh breeze wiping out three years of pain and drama could not resist bad faith. Ariel Sharon does not even try any more to make the change; the construction of the wall will go on, Palestinian lands will continue to be stolen, frontiers to be changed and neighbouring Arab countries to be attacked in a move that is changing the whole fragile environment of the region. The only thing not to change is the Bush Administration policy: it will do nothing. "The wall creates a problem", but the next US electoral campaign will not be concerned by this "problem". Sharon can peacefully continue to bomb Syria, and maybe tomorrow Iran. The US will not move and Sharon knows it. "Israel cannot have the liberty to destroy here and there and expect the Arab side to keep silent," said Arab League Moussa after the Syrian bombing. Yes Israel can, and it knows it. As Sharon recently said, "Israel will strike in every place and with any means."

Elsewhere, distorted information goes on fooling the people. "Intelligence information was made sexier" in the UK and the 45-minute argument (where Tony Blair said that Saddam Hussein's weapons of mass destruction "were actionable in 45 minutes") was false? No problem; Prime Minister Tony Blair has no reverse gear. US experts have just presented their report which confirms there were no weapons of mass destruction in Iraq? "David Kay still has a long work to do," answers President Bush's think-tank Condoleezza Rice. (David Kay was the head of the US mission which searched for the presences of WMDs to no avail.) For once, she might be telling the truth: it is likely that many more years will be needed by a 1400-strong team of experts who could not find anything after six months. It is also true to say that with a new allocated budget of US$600 million, one may end up finding something.

Meanwhile, Bush will send the UN to hell: "Give me your money, and I'll take care of it." In the meantime, he will ask for an additional US$87 billion from Congress. As an economist put it recently, US$350 spent in Iraq for US$1 against AIDS. It's all a question of priorities. As far as Iraq is concerned, one could even say "family first". Jim Hoagland, from the *Washington Post* said it: "The Bush Administration needs to remember Rule One of crisis behaviour: when you are in a hole, stop digging."

All these people do whatever they want because there is no sanction, no counterweight, even though, as Philip Stephens wrote in the *Financial Times*, "We see that 'Pax Americana' no longer seems quite so impregnable a construct." This is the reason why one should be more attentive to the possible results of the International Government Conference (CIG), which opened last week [4 October 2003] in Rome. As one knows, this conference was gathered for the EU governments to approve a "constitution" which will be substituted in all existing treaties regulating the functioning of Europe. This 200-page document is the result of an 18-month-long preliminary work headed by the former French President Valery Giscard d'Estaing. It is obviously a compromise between different cultures, practices and feelings, and it cannot please everybody in the same way; governments, according to Giscard, should accept it as it is; otherwise they run the risk of dismantling the whole work.

As one might expect, it already gave way to a significant number of discussions on several technical issues, which quickly became political. And as one might also expect, two leading contestants are two of the US's staunchest allies: Spain and Rumsfeld's new darling, Poland. There are four main points under discussion: the number of commissioners (to be reduced to 15 on a rotating basis); the weighting of votes (50 per cent of the member states and 60 per cent of the EU population, which results in a minority blockage option for the largest countries); the definition of practical steps towards a strengthening of the European defence (with the UK unexpectedly agreeing to implement structured co-operations), and a reference to the Christian values of the EU history, which is not an insuperable issue. It is likely that these points will give way to endless discussions, but that a solution will finally emerge, unless Spain and Poland take the risk of failure. It is not sure this is to their advantage: besides the fact that both countries have been, or are going to be, among the largest beneficiaries of EU structural aid for development, they should understand, as the Belgium Foreign Affairs Minister Louis Michel said, that "they can't get the butter and the money that goes with it". Poland (a country where France is the largest foreign investor) has everything to lose from not joining the EU, especially because of the subsidies it hopes to receive for its agriculture. However, it will be no loss for the other countries in the EU if it does not make it.

In any event, the true question doesn't lie there. Whatever the fate of the CIG, the essence is the capacity for a few members to start teaming up more closely and move forward at their own pace even though others would be more reluctant to follow suit. This two-step approach is a must in the face of present challenges. Europe has to reform its political, economical and social systems; it has to take the necessary measures to re-acquire a plain sovereignty through an independent security and pledge the necessary financial resources for that. Europe has considerable means, but those are split incoherently between too many actors. The new constitution should correct this. Finally, Europe needs an independent defence. The EU is not just a huge supermarket where people do their shopping and defer to others every time they feel threatened. This is the sense of the Berlin–Paris axis to which you can add Belgium, Luxembourg and perhaps one day the UK in spite of Germany and France having been waiting 25 years for that. As former Minister Hubert Vedrine recently said: "Self-proclaimed hard cores may not be viable because Europe has always moved forward thanks to differentiation; yet, we have to be present in each and every innovating combination until it is seen that an advanced guard has emerged." In the meantime, Europe has to fight against a declining population, insufficient research and development, and a lack of growth-generating investments. This is enough to make the main countries of Europe gather and work together at co-ordinated solutions before the ongoing internationalisation of the Middle East conflict puts the whole world deeper at risk.

WHY IS THE WORLD SO BAD?

28 October 2003

For the first time since the end of the Second World War, the world is getting closer to waters that may prove far more dangerous than those of the Cold War and other conflicts it has lived through in the past 50 years. When the usual guide-marks tend to disappear, the fact that sources of different conflicts seem to be merging in the same Middle East area is raising the risk of deflagration. But it may not be due to Al Qaida. The present state of international relationships is marked by what happened on 11 September 2001. Not because it was the beginning of a new era – rather it is a landmark on a long road that had started with the rise of Islamic fundamentalism – but because it appeared as the signal the Bush Administration needed to launch its planned attack against Iraq. Now it has done it alone, the only question of interest for the rest of the world is to know what their next step is. This is where possible answers become cause for concern.

A first aspect of the Bush policy is marked by the belief that international law and multilateral organisations pose a direct threat to America's sovereignty and ability to defend itself. A result is that its hegemonic situation has gradually led it to isolate itself in a world that has little to do with the complex reality. To sum it up, "there is nothing else in the world more important than American security" and "who is not with us is against us"; hence a unilateral policy reflecting a hegemonic behaviour whereby each nation should define itself in terms of its relationship with the US. A consequence of this Cold War-inspired policy, as if Condoleezza Rice was not aware of the wall's collapse in Berlin, is that while the US wastes significant time in identifying friends and foes, they do not tackle the problems. As the economist Jeffrey Sachs says: "Because they see every problem through the lens of terror, they consider themselves excused from the global struggle against poverty and disease." The Bush policy shows that Americans can now be constrained and led by fear whereas, writes Professor Peter Sloterdijk, "the refusal of tragedy used to constitute the foundation act of the Motherland of the second chance". The US have lost their faith and they are losing their friends. Of course, this situation reflects on the Transatlantic Alliance. Past US administrations used to think that whatever happened to it, the US national interest was better served by a cohesive Europe. On the contrary, the show of strength now supersedes the respect for friends and the "divide and rule" attitude makes Dick Cheney and Donald Rumsfeld believe, writes Quentin Peel in the *Financial Times*, that "American hegemony is better served by a fractured Europe from which they can select coalitions of the willing".

This background is necessary to understanding what is presently taking place in the Middle East, especially in the two well-known areas for concern, Palestine and Iraq, now extending to Syria and Iran. Regarding Palestine, there is nothing new to say that is not already known, as confirmed last week when the contents of the 'Geneva Initiative' led by the Israeli Yossi Beilin and the Palestinian Yasser Abed Rabbo, emerged: Israeli withdrawal to 1987 borders, dismantling of the colonies which are deep inside Palestine, sharing of control over Jerusalem with international presence allowing free access to everybody; adjusted recognition of the right of return and shut-down of radical Islamic groups. A growing perception that an international force is a compulsory element to the one-shot implementation of a peace agreement in Palestine, any step-by-step approach having proven unworkable, is also comforting. As former Israeli Ambassador to Paris, Elia Barhavi, said: "Internationalisation of the conflict is the only solution; the military option is unable to reduce terrorism; ultra-patriots who are now governing Israel are digging the tomb of the Jewish State." But Prime Minister Sharon is also "a major obstacle to the road to peace" and dismissed the attempt a few days before the US did likewise. Actually, Sharon may simply have misunderstood Barhavi: "internationalisation of the conflict" did not mean "exporting the conflict" – what he tried to do in bombing Syria, which was also a clear signal to Iran, rather, it was an attempt to export the Palestinian conflict to the whole of the Middle East region. The main success of Oslo was to uncouple this conflict from the overall Arab relationship with the rest of the world. This new development is also taking place when the situation is significantly worsening in Iraq, mostly because of the American incompetence (inability to manage the post-war security, administration and engineering fields), and partly because of the ongoing shift of attitude of the Shia community. A UN resolution will change nothing, a reason why it was unanimously accepted. Last week's [23/24 October 2003] donor countries' conference in Madrid allowed the US not to lose face, even though (as with Spain) less than 10 per cent of the pledged amounts will reach the Reconstruction Fund.[1] Bush family friends will be able to go on with their tricky business, according to US Representative Waxman.

Despite all that, this is when the Bush Administration resumes its campaign against Iran. "Bin Laden's son plays a big role in directing Al Qaida from Iran", blows the *Wall Street Journal*, whose reporter surely met Bin Laden in the Teheran-based Al Qaida Inc. head office building. In a Cold War-like remake, Nobel Peace Prize winner Shirin Ebadi, like Poland's Lech Walesa, "will make Iran tumble" (wasn't Arafat also a Prize winner?) as in Iraq "where the US are trying to establish a democratic, pro-western bulwark in the heart of the terror-breeding ground that is today the Middle East" so the US may be tempted by a new adventure in Iran. Sharon also may be tempted by them, as Israeli Intelligence's voluntarily leaked 'Harpoon story'[2] may suggest in these unilateral times of pre-emptive strikes. The US Middle East policy used to be balanced on two legs, the oil policy and support to Israel. This second leg has obviously taken over and the Middle East is becoming the centre of all dangers. After an Iraq war begun in total disrespect of any prevailing international rules of law, will the US ring the bell or smash down the door of Iran? The international community can legitimately ask this question.

NOTES

1 On 23 and 24 October 2003, one week after UN resolution 1511 authorising a US multilateral force in Iraq was passed, the US organised a "donors conference" in Madrid where it gathered 73 countries and 20 international organisations. The scope of the conference was to raise money to fund the reconstruction of Iraq. Officially, $33 billion were raised – out of which however, 20 were to come from the US government but were still under discussion in Congress. Ultimately, $3 to 7 billion only were pledged from non-US sources. Claimed as a "political success" by the Bush Administration, in reality the conference did not have many concrete results.

2 In the course of October 2003, Israeli intelligence voluntarily leaked confidential information about the Israeli technical capacity to launch the so-called Israeli-made 'harpoon missiles' as far as Iran.

A FAREWELL TO LAW

10 November 2003

Did America ever realise it was returning to the cradle of civilisation on reaching Mesopotamia? It went back 3000 years anyway, as far as law versus absolute strength is concerned. America today is at war with Iraq not to fight criminals or terrorism but because it has an interest in it: a revenge interest as a result of September 11 (although no link with Al Qaida was ever proven); a security interest, although they could not find weapons of mass destruction; a faith interest because, as President Bush has said, "Iraq is a part of a global democratic revolution." The Bush Administration has many motives to stay where it is and the way it calls its war will change nothing, provided it can justify a military occupation and a landmark for juicy contracts.

The lawless unilateral decision of the Bush Administration to declare war on Iraq was supposed to be legitimised afterwards. History shows it often happens to illegal actions that are successful. Yet it did not happen with Iraq, where the situation worsens everyday. Let's put aside bombings, the civilian dead and wounded, infrastructure destruction and post-war management incompetence; let us focus on daily realities: "Wouldn't you react if your country was invaded?" a man in the street was heard telling the press. The rest is insignificant. Establishing a distinction among daily attacks between military, Al Qaida or nationalist actions is indeed of very little value after listening to an Iraqi child collecting the debris of a crashed Chinook helicopter in Fallujah: "I'll keep the bits and give them to Saddam when he comes back"! What will Donald Rumsfeld or Paul Wolfowitz's incantations about their willingness "to achieve our mission in Iraq which is precisely to get rid of this type of criminal and to invite the world to fight against the new alliance of Saddam supporters and international terrorism" do as long as cheering crowds dance in the street when a US helicopter crashes? The Bush Administration is leading a war in Iraq which, incidentally, it is not winning in spite of the unforgettable words of Bush: "The more progress we achieve on the field, the more ferocious attacks we shall face." American soldiers in Iraq, albeit hidden behind their concrete walls with no contact with the local population, are foreigners. Those fighting them are mainly Iraqis, be they Iraqi terrorists or Iraqi resistance. (Since the Second World War, every occupying army has called a terrorist a resistance fighter.) In the meantime, US soldiers "bunkerise" themselves and become increasingly distant and anxious, whereas reconstruction actions slide away and resentment increases. Yet they will not change.

They will not even share the slightest responsibility – for instance, trusting the Iraqis with keeping the security. "Let the Iraqis take care themselves of their own security and you will see that they know how to do it," said the Najaf Governor to Paul Bremer recently. But this is denied to Iraqis. The US will not give up a nail until they get back a satisfactory return on investment. They call it "implementing democracy", but everybody understands. Choking down a sob, the *Wall Street Journal* was recently complaining that: "Rather than report on Saddam Hussein torturers, journalists care only about Halliburton's contracts."[1] It would indeed be so easy to leave them and others to carry on reaping what they can of the country and put it up for auction. Even a former World Bank official sounded the alarm as to the way the occupying Administration rules the issue of privatisation, with no technology transfer and little training: "Before privatisation, you need a government, a functioning Finance Ministry and real security." A recent [3 November 2003] lawyers' conference in London warned that many aspects of this process may be illegal simply because they are contrary to local law and constitution. But America doesn't care because international law doesn't apply to it. In modern times, when one started a crusade, prior consent of the international community was required. "In an open world, no one can live in isolation, no one can act alone in the name of all," President Jacques Chirac said. This was echoed by Chancellor Gerhard Schroeder to whom "security in today's world cannot be guaranteed by one country going it alone". Joining together was the way countries found themselves organising their relationship if it could not be founded on strength only. The place for that is the UN, which was supposed to become "insignificant" if it would not support the US in Iraq, although it still remains the place today.

This is why the "global fight against terrorism" becomes a justification for everything and this is when the legitimate question of the "right of intervention" is raised, a matter often characterised by cowardliness and hypocrisy. Who would pretend that Saddam Hussein was not a terrible dictator and that the world is surely better off without him? Yet was his case an isolated one, and can one country act alone according to its own values especially when the 45-minute deployment time of weapons of mass destruction, and indeed the weapons of mass destruction themselves, proved false? Attacks take place daily in Iraq, even if they are "co-ordinated", come from many sources and the terrorist alibi is an intellectual shame: terrorism is a multifaceted reality yet the term is often used in undiscerning ways. What should one think, for instance, of a country that holds 680 prisoners from 42 countries in 2.5 metre-square aluminium cells with no indictment, no judgement and no Geneva protection because they are not recognised as "prisoners of war" but merely "combatant enemies"? This is happening in an American-controlled territory in Guantanamo (Cuba). Continuing to call both Iraqi nationalists or Saddam supporters "terrorists", mixing up international terrorism, religious fanatics, liberation movements or occupied populations fighting a foreign presence on their land will actually only result in diverting forces and fighting none of them efficiently. Because of this, international co-operation will fail: another reason why fighting terrorism this way will not work. Another step is now emerging with the "forward strategy of freedom in the Middle East", what President Bush calls "the establishment of a free Iraq at the heart of the Middle East which will be a watershed event in the global democratic revolution". The point, however, is that the US are only interested in their leaderships regardless of their commitment to democracy. "No one believes the US is genuine," says Jordan University's Harmane, especially in front of US endorsement of Israel's continued abuse of Palestinian rights. There may be a solution, reminds Philip Stephens in the *Financial Times*, as "only a political settlement between Israel and Palestine will erode the visceral mistrust of the US". But this is not new; it was written by the US envoy in Baghdad, in 1952.

NOTES

1. The Halliburton company is the mother company of the US engineering group Kellog Brown Root, an entity in a rather poor financial condition. The company was awarded contracts in Iraq without any open competition being organised. US Vice President Dick Cheney was Chairman of the company from 1995 until 2000. Another scandal hit the company when it appeared during the fall of 2003 that it had outrageously overpriced imported gasoline in Iraq that was on-sold to the American army.

WILL THE US ALLOW EUROPE TO BECOME AN ADULT?

24 November 2003

States are cold-blooded monsters that only have interests. This is why they normally care about their own people, protect them, help them to gain new markets or extend influence and, usually, care little about others, as the US has done in Iraq. So why is US behaviour becoming so odious to an increasing part of the world? Probably because of a pretension that whatever they do, they do it for the world rather than for themselves. They did not fight in Vietnam to maintain their presence in South East Asia, they fought communism; they did not invade Iraq to expand their presence in the Middle East, they fight terrorism. This is also why they will never win the war over terrorism for democracy, for the definition of their target is biased: whoever doesn't think as they do is a "terrorist". Democracy is their only view on the way powers should be organised; a kind of a variable geometry colonial democracy.

This behaviour should be remembered when reviewing the emerging independent European defence issue. EU members assume defence through its own army and the North Atlantic Treaty Organisation, NATO. Effectively, NATO is in the hands of the US which provides most of the equipment and assumes the highest commanding responsibilities; the civilian head of NATO is usually non-American. However, most of the EU states, except the UK and France, do not have the means to build an independent defence force. In addition to them, the new members of the EU will find with NATO the kind of safety belt that could protect them. Yet if Europe is to become a political entity with an autonomous power, it needs strength to support it. Especially if Donald Rumsfeld's words – "It is not a coalition which commands the mission but the mission which commands a coalition" – mean the death of NATO's classical role. The US arguments "Why do you need to build up something which already exists?" has the same limited value as, "Why do you need to manufacture Airbus aircraft as we can provide you with Boeing?" Independence means capacity of choice and Europe may have different choices to the US for whom anything opposing hegemony is considered as antagonist. As Henry Kissinger said: "It is necessary that countries do not lead their foreign policy as if their first objective was to put an end to this unavoidable evidence of the American military superiority." Keep quiet and move away. Europe has set up a paper framework into which security and defence mechanisms should be organised. A joint declaration by France and the UK in Saint Malo in 1998 says that Europe must have the means to play its role on the international stage, and that includes an autonomy backed by credible military forces and the means to decide to use them. Since the framework was designed, it was now time to become practical and allocate the necessary means and resources to achieve such goals. The setting up of a European integrated planning defence headquarters is one of them.

Alas, British policy these days seems to depend on who was on the phone last and the practical implementation of an autonomous defence has been vigorously attacked by the US and a US-led diffuse opposition by EU newcomers. What is the story all about? A joint proposal by Belgium, France, Germany and Luxembourg in April 2003 to set up a European integrated defence planning headquarters, distinct from NATO's HQ. NATO's reaction was swift: "We do not think it is useful to improve military capacities, notably because such a structure already exists within NATO or at the national level," said UK Defence Minister Geoff Hoon. Why Airbus? We already have Boeing! Even Tony Blair appeared to have said one day that "the European Union should be endowed with a joint capacity to plan and conduct operations without recourse to NATO resources and capabilities", and that is what happened recently in Macedonia and in DR Congo.

A more global approach is emerging from the new European constitution draft which provides for the capacity to join forces for whichever member wishes it. This two-step or avant-garde approach allows for members who desire it to go faster and deeper into the union. Some European countries who are not prepared to assume their own destiny and pay the price for it may prefer the sole American umbrella, but why should other countries be prevented from teaming up? Actually, Europe as the second world economic power and a growing political power will necessarily develop a European defence, and the recent agreement to set up a new defence agency, which will co-ordinate military purchases, is the first step in this direction. If the UK joins, the move will be swifter.

If if doesn't, its belonging to the EU will ultimately be at stake. So it will join, because it is in its interest. For sure, "America today is the truth and light for Tony Blair", who himself adds that: "Whatever others may say, most people know that our alliance with America and our position in Europe give us unparalleled purchase on international affairs for a country of our size." He may be right regarding the size of the country but as for the rest, what kind of "purchase" is he referring to? Being informed by the American ally one hour before strikes? Being told by Rumsfeld that finally "the US might well have done it without the British"? Benefiting from special treatment for UK prisoners in Guantanamo? Being heard about the environment, steel levies or Palestine? For which reasons would the US be entitled to forbid the EU to implement "strengthened co-operations" and at the same time warn about the risk of "a giant recluse freed of his friends and advisors" when the Bush Administration cronies start any editorial with formulas such as "US former allies and friends France and Germany"? "The biggest threat to the Atlantic Alliance is not the progress of European Defence. What would really threaten its future would be a weak, divided Europe, abdicating its responsibilities. 'Europe Defence' will progress because it is a necessity for everyone who wants a strong Europe and a lasting alliance." This was written by Kissinger, who cannot be seen as a strong supporter of an independent Europe. For sure, a new transatlantic partnership where "one should escape from a dilemma between a relationship based upon command and obeisance and a relationship based upon opposition or rivalry" (Pierre Hassner) should be drafted; but a first step is to have minimal power before talking to whoever recognises strength only. Let's hope that on the occasion of the UK–France Summit at Lancaster House, London [24 November 2003], Blair will realise that the UK is no more an island.

TIME TO GET RID OF THE PLAGUE OF NEO-COLONIAL DEMOCRACY

8 December 2003

A Holy War for democracy has just been launched by US President George W. Bush. From his "Shrine to democracy" – the Oval office – on 13 November he set the terms of a "Forward strategy of freedom". The reasons for leading a war into Iraq – the presence of weapons of mass destruction and a link with Al Qaida – were never proven. Yet the US will bring democracy to Arab states that do not know what it is. "There is no democracy in Arab countries," summed up Iraqi expert Amir Taheri in his usual subtle way. The good news for him is the confirmation of the fact by Israeli Ambassador Shlomo Avineri: "Of the 22 member states of the Arab League, none is a democracy or on the way to becoming one." The bad news, adds Avineri, is:

> The new timetable in Iraq attests the degree of desperation felt in Washington, but it is no more likely to succeed than earlier US plans: to imagine that the first functioning institutional democracy in the Arab world will flourish on the Euphrates, backed up by American buyout, is a dangerous illusion.

But this is not to subdue the faith of Taheri-like crusaders: "In at least 30 Muslim countries, terrorism – be it practised by the state or by its opponents – is an integrated part of any political life; there is terrorism wherever there is no democracy." Even though a striking characteristic of the presence of two "democratic" countries in the Middle East is a colonial occupation – the US one in Iraq and the Israeli one in Palestine – the fight for democracy will supersede any other political aim. It was obviously never intended by the rich and mighty that through colossal military means a new geo-policy conformed with their countries' respective interests.

A problem with the simplest analyses is that they often go wrong. Globalising the threat, as the Bush Administration is doing, leads to globalising the answer. Yet the threat is as diversified as any answer to it. There is Islamic terrorism, but not all terrorists are Muslims and not all Arabs are Muslims and all Muslims are not terrorists. Many liberation movements are only considered terrorists until they obtain power and become rulers. The matter is thus complex, but it is not the worse for it. "Internationally, US actions speak louder than words," writes Quentin Peel in the *Financial Times*. Undoubtedly, this is where the Bush concept of democracy may leave a few democrats perplexed.

Interesting examples were given in this newspaper [*Gulf News*] by Patrick Seale (a regular commentator): an illegitimate dictatorship in Syria and in Iran where the US Administration gave a helping hand to overthrow people legitimately elected; democratic freedom in Iraq where 20,000 civilians and soldiers were killed and 30,000 wounded; prisoners in Guantanamo "who are entitled to be fed, sheltered and clothed but not entitled to a timetable requiring their release or trial before the terrorist organisation for which they fight has been destroyed" dare to write two "Washington DC lawyers" in the *Wall Street Journal*; Palestinians who are not authorised to work and feed their families while Israelis steal their lands. But this is not all, and without coming back to El Salvador and other Vietnams, how can anybody seriously take into consideration the Bush Administration's search for democracy when the State Department's Richard Armitage (the US Deputy Secretary of State) stops in Azerbaijan to congratulate Alieyev Junior who won after a massive fraud; when international treaties are for others but never for them; what to think of "an almost invisible president hidden by phalanxes of security men" when visiting London, this new Imperator of a democratic universe who cannot even leave the glass bubble into which he protects himself from loving and cheering crowds? "We will win because our cause is just," says the man who leaves his ranch in an unmarked car, travels incognito, takes off and lands in total darkness and talks to the only people who seem to be able to listen without harming him. Everything seems fake, including the turkey.

One would even wish to widen the matter further. "The US constitution", wrote Paul Barry last summer in *Politique Internationale* magazine "is based upon the French Montesquieu's philosophy of a balance between three powers rigorously separated – the legislative, judiciary and executive powers. The reason for Roman decadence was to rely on the last one, the military executive power of the Imperator, with no other counter-power. The stubbornness of the Bush Administration to write-off any counter-power from the planet is a threat to the constitutional spirit and thus the democratic basis itself of the United States." Was it therefore possible, not to say desirable, to export democracy in Iraq? Some, as does the *Financial Times*, will say that "the prize of legitimacy far outweighs the US preference for a top-down strategy built around favoured exiles and a timetable synchronised with the Bush re-election campaign" and will consequently call for a constitution written by an assembly directly elected by all Iraqis and not indirectly elected by a gathering of notables as Paul Bremer wishes. This will lead to a situation in which a majority of Shia will rule over Sunni as no true democracy can, as is the case in Iraq, contest its own majority. Others will say that American democracy is not suitable for export, as the experience in Latin America[1] has shown. As Denis Lacorne writes:

> A simple democratic system based upon one man, one vote will, in Iraq, ensure the end of the democratic experience and the implementation of a Shia theocracy. A true democracy remains to be set in place: a complex system of weighted votes, protected minorities, redesigned territories, a system which finally may be existing only in Switzerland!

What appears in any event is that the Arab states do not seem willing to be colonised by an external way of life based on "universal values" whose interpretation is biased. They favour freedom over tyrannical rules; they want Arab and Muslim aspirations to be taken into account instead of a status being imposed on them that is nothing else but the reflection of a neo-colonial behaviour. Both the western and Muslim worlds can meet together around a commonly accepted minimal ethical basis. But this can only be achieved through mutual respect and reciprocal knowledge — two virtues that have been absent from the White House these last years.

NOTES

1 The various attempts by America to help implement democracy in Latin America have generally resulted in outright opposition from the concerned populations (Nicaragua), invasions (Panama) and direct or indirect interventions aimed at imposing its policy (12-year civil war in El Salvador, Iran-Contra scandal in Honduras against Nicaragua, etc.). Another characteristic is passive behaviour in front of obvious attempts on basic democratic principles (in Chile, Argentina, El Salvador for example). Furthermore, unclear US reactions vis-à-vis drug smuggling or arms trading with official governments or rebels in the region have darkened the overall perception of the situation.

WORLD HEADLINES: EITHER TOO SWEET OR TOO SOUR

22 December 2003

At a time when the Bush Administration makes dates bloom in winter, one should be careful about what one reads. Sticking to the last two weeks' headlines, Saddam Hussein's "recent" capture should change the course of the war in Iraq; peace could be within reach in Occupied Palestine and the apparent failure of the latest EU summit in Brussels would be a significant drawback for the new 25-member Europe. So what?

Saddam's capture, whenever it took place, will actually change few of the numerous issues that the American occupation army face in Iraq. One may complain that once again the Bush Administration tried to mislead the public, by seizing a haggard Saddam; an American soldier pointing his gun at a hole with a bunch of yellow dates behind his shoulder looked as genuine as a magnificent roasted turkey. One may also object to the fact that despite a thorough medical examination and humiliating-or-not shave, no weapons of mass destruction were found in Saddam's ears nor Osama bin Laden's mobile phone number in his pockets. What is certain, however, is that besides the many people who continued to die in several attacks the very day Saddam was arrested, he did not look like the one co-ordinating the resistance. A dictator being captured is excellent news. "His days are finished," President Bush said, adding that Saddam deserved both the death penalty and a "fair" trial. Yet his arrest did not lead to finding any weapons of mass destruction. The manner in which the Saddam issue was handled may have been "a message telling Arab leaders that he who doesn't enter the poultry yard of the Americans will experience the same fate", as the Egyptian writer Sayed Nassar put it. But still, the main issue remains: who will elect the representatives of the Iraqi people who are supposed to draft a new constitution? How will the US tackle the existing Shia majority issue? How long will the occupying army be able to pump Iraqi oil, sell it to the markets and make money without any international reaction? German,

French or Russian companies are forbidden from bidding for Iraqi reconstruction contracts. The US Deputy Defence Secretary Paul Wolfowitz said: "It was necessary for protecting the essential security interests of the US to limit competition." The former US Secretary of State James Baker toured Europe and Russia seeking Iraqi debt write-offs. The US investment in Iraq has started to pay rewards, if not for "the American tax payers" then at least for those "initial participating firms". Anyhow, the situation in Iraq has become such a mess that Americans can only look for an exit strategy. The cost of the war and daily casualties are becoming an embarrassment in an electoral year. Partition proposals of the country are so much favoured by Israel that nobody may even look at them: the only solution, everyone knows, is to bring the international community back into the picture.

In Geneva, there are Palestinians and Israelis who can talk to each other. But any implementation of a peace agreement will have to be imposed by an international power, since every gradual approach has proved unworkable. Geneva is just another step in a never-ending discussion about stolen lands to be given back by thieves who are more powerful than their victims. Exhausted Palestinians now seem prepared to accept anything, like the shepherds of Jayousgota who just want to take their sheep to their meadows on the other side of the barrier. But Israeli soldiers forbid them from doing so. The sheep have no permits, they say. When animals are kept away from pastures legally owned by their shepherds, what worse can happen?

A more positive note emerged from the apparent European failure over future voting powers in the EU. One could complain that Poland should not have imposed its own views on a club it was just joining: apart from the US, nobody, indeed, is forcing Poland to join the European Union. Belgian, French or Dutch agriculture is better off without Poland. As for Spain, the largest beneficiary of European aid, a direct link with the *Wall Street Journal*'s Europe editor may have temporarily led this country to lose a sense of reality. In spite of the subtle support of the UK's Prime Minister Tony Blair, Spain nevertheless tried and failed. This is excellent news as there are now no more hurdles to the "pioneer group" concept of moving ahead. Among the many possible Europes, two are confronting each other: the one favoured by the US which calls for the emergence of a large market only where US goods and influence will expand freely; the other which calls for a powerful Europe that will define its own strategy, take the means for it and start teaming up with countries sharing a common vision in fields as different as defence, crime or immigration. There may still be a long way to go before such a Confederation of Nation States takes root and some countries may have already given up. Others have not and a two-speed Europe is an answer because results can be more easily achieved with 5 than 25. One should thus be grateful to Spain and Poland to have offered the original founder members of the Union (with or without Italy, who knows?) the historic opportunity to focus on the only true issue: not how Europe should be organised but what it wants to be and to do. Failing to define and develop a strategy for a powerful Europe will indeed offer no other alternative in ten years than to transform our countries into genuine Disneylands.

2004

OLD WARS, NEW WARS

Timeline World News 2004

11 March:	Almost 200 people are killed and more than 1000 injured in Madrid, when several bombs explode on morning commuter trains.
22 March:	Historical Hamas leader Sheikh Yassin is assassinated by the Israeli army.
12 April:	New Hamas leader Dr Abdulaziz Rantissi is assassinated by the Israeli army.
28 April:	Photos released of prisoners at Abu Ghraib prison being abused by US soldiers.
23 May:	Gathering of Arab Heads of State in Tunis.
5 June:	Former US Republican President Ronald Reagan dies, aged 93.
10 June:	D-Day celebrations.
September:	Larry Franklin, a US engineer, is found guilty of passing secret information to Israel.
1 September:	Nearly 1000 children are held hostage by Chechen militants at their school. The three-day siege ended with nearly 300 people (half of whom were children) being killed.
9 October:	In Afghanistan, the country's first elections result in Hamid Karzai becoming president.
31 October:	The Ukrainian elections end in turmoil among accusations of fraud.
November:	Viktor Yanukovych is elected President of Ukraine, but result is overuled by the Ukrainian Parliament.
11 November:	Yasser Arafat, leader of the Palestine Liberation Organisation, dies in a French hospital, aged 75.
December:	A re-run of the Ukraine elections results in Viktor Yushchenko, who claimed he had been poisoned during the election campaign, becoming president.
26 December:	Indian Ocean suffers massive tsunami, leaving hundreds of thousands dead, and uncountable numbers homeless.

A YEAR ALL OUT OF LIES, LIES AND MORE LIES

5 JANUARY 2004

The year 2003 started with a hoax about weapons of mass destruction in Iraq and ended with a bogeyman in Libya. But still, both the US and the world are not any safer because of it.

Indeed, 2003 will be remembered as a year of lies, not only because the motives for the war in Iraq were dubious and the facts distorted, but also because the prime minister of the oldest western democracy bluntly lied in Parliament about Iraq's capability to launch deadly missile attacks within a 45-minute period. Additionally, the Secretary of State of the wealthiest western democracy blatantly lied at the UN about Iraqi weapons of mass destruction hidden in storage places "which can't even be communicated to allies for security reasons". However, nobody was able to find any such weapons after the invasion. Such misleading statements, which cost the lives of many Iraqis and coalition troops since "the war ended", would normally have led to resignations in democratic countries.

Let's forget about Saddam Hussein's capture, which was said to be a "turning point" in a war that is proving to be increasingly silly with each passing day. Let's dismiss the "revival of a normal civic life in Iraq", which is not true, or "avoiding the partition of the country", which can still happen. The real question is this: is the world better off as a result of the war against Iraq? The answer is obviously no. A dictator was deposed, which is excellent news, but there are still many others around. It is hardly conceivable that a war will be launched against all of them. Christians continue to be massacred in Sudan and pregnant North Korean women continue to face forced abortion if they try and fail to leave their country. There is no oil in Sudan or in North Korea. Historian Bernard Lewis has recently claimed that "respect for America has only increased with its demonstration of strength and purpose". One should offer him a ticket to London the next time President Bush visits the city. As Britain's *Financial Times* mentioned: "Just imagine how much people around the world would demonstrate against Bush's policies, looking at the number of Brits who took to the streets." A more worrying element is the growing imperial approach of the US, as perfectly described in the editorial in America's *Wall Street Journal* on 2 January:

> Another global benefit of the war is the end of the illusions about the UN and a certain kind of "multilateralism" ... The lesson of Iraq is that only the US has the political will and military means to defeat global threats. American Presidents in the future will likewise have to build coalition on an ad hoc basis, often working around a UN Security Council obstructed by France.

This is the usual rhetoric from the neo-conservative and ultra-Zionist lobbies and the premise for future dictatorships. Yet the same administration on the same day showed a different side through its Secretary of State in the French daily *Le Figaro*: "Are we accused of being unilateralist? This is not true. Do we favour military means? Not at all. Is our strategy obsessed with terrorism, leading us to carry out pre-emptive strikes? This is totally erroneous." Whom to believe?

In any event, two things are certain. First, as long as the Bush Administration believes that Iraq is integral to the war on terror, terrorism will continue. Is the world really safer today when the entire US is placed on an "orange alert" and violence is a daily reality in the Middle East? The truth is that the occupation of Iraq has re-launched terrorism and made the place receptive to it, notably because an occupation can never become an act of liberation without legitimacy. John Paul II said in his Christmas address: "A victorious fight against terrorism cannot be limited to repression and punishment. It must be accompanied by a courageous and lucid analysis of the underlying motives of the attacks."

Second, it was wrong to assume that a regime change in Iraq would become a springboard for the resumption of serious talks to resolve the Middle East dispute. "The Israeli government of Ariel Sharon has hidden behind the lethal assumption that it can dictate the terms of any peace with the Palestinians," wrote Philip Stephens in the *Financial Times*, even before Sharon spoke of a new plan to build 900 houses in Occupied Golan Heights as an answer to Syrian President Bashar Al Assad's proposal to resume peace talks. More widely, democracy itself is not emerging unscathed from the Iraqi misadventure. Of course, there is Guantanamo; but there is also Libya like a cherry on the top.

"Colonel [Muammar] Gaddafi needs to be applauded in unqualified terms, as he has shown huge statesmanship," British Foreign Secretary Jack Straw dared to declare, thus joining a group of mentally deficient zombies. Quentin Peel put it aptly in the *Financial Times*: "Such adjectives seem incredibly inappropriate." It is indeed an ironically cruel coincidence that the first democratic achievement of President Bush's "forward strategy for freedom in the Middle East" be the recognition of a bogeyman who paid the Lockerbie victims' families US$2.7 billion to make up for 35 years of absolute dictatorship and sponsoring all kinds of terrorism. But success with Iran against proliferation of weapons of mass destruction had too much of a European flavour and the Bush Administration needed something more. In the wait for George and Tony to visit their friend Muammar in Tripoli next summer, Israeli Defence Minister General Saül Mofaz threatened to bomb Iranian nuclear installations in a pre-emptive strike. At least the Arabs will now know where Gaddafi stands.

Neo-conservatives intend to change the world according to their own beliefs and bring "culture" to countries that were merely able to build cities such as Damascus and Isfahan. In doing that, as Martin Wolf wrote in the *Financial Times*, they have "humiliated allies, undermined international institutions and projected a narrow vision of US interests". This is why Harvard University's Carr Professor of Human Rights Practice Michael Ignatieff thinks that a war against terror without friends and allies will fail: because "the Achilles heel of American power has been its inability to understand its dependence on others".

WHEN IT COMES TO TRANSPARENCY ...

18 JANUARY 2004

"What is charming me is uncertainty. Everything becomes marvellous in the mist," Oscar Wilde once noted. Whether US President Bush is going to win another mandate or not is of limited interest to those who cannot do anything about it. However, showing what this administration has been able to do in the past three years is far more instructive. For years, many analysts have regarded Bush as a pale imitation of his father. He is seen as a kind of rich families' inheritor with few brains and many advisors, and a very average level of studies, a rather poor general understanding of culture, obvious difficulties in speaking in public without confusing his words or making gaffes, a tumultuous early private life before redemption, and a lacklustre professional career before getting into politics. Bush and his advisors may not be stars, but more, perhaps, "a blind man in a room full of deaf people", to quote Bush's former Treasury Secretary Paul O'Neill.

However, one must always be cautious about the comments of aides fired by their former bosses. Resentment of disgruntled ex-employees is never far behind. Yet an interesting point in O'Neill's comment is precisely what Britain's *Financial Times* reproached him for: "O'Neill feels duped; his latest tirade shows him to be not only disloyal but also naive – a far more serious offence." Presenting Bush as "disengaged, intellectually shallow and uninterested in economic policy" is nothing new. Underlying the role played by US Vice President Dick Cheney in the second round of tax cuts in 2002 offers some interesting clues about the former Halliburton chief's influence in White House policy. But affirming that Bush plotted to remove Saddam Hussein from power and occupy Iraq from the day he took office is, undoubtedly, something new. This is not because it confirms that Saddam was "Topic A" in the first meeting of the National Security Council (NSC) in January 2001, but because the NSC discussed an occupation of Iraq as early as January 2001 – well before 9/11. What followed was just "fixing", like in boxing or horse racing. "I never saw anything that I would characterise as evidence of weapons of mass destruction ... From the very beginning, there was a conviction; it was all about finding a way to do it. The President saying 'Go find me a way to do this.'" These words were not the ones we heard from Colin Powell at the UN.

There were no weapons of mass destruction, there was no link to Al Qaida, there was no immediate threat either – yet the Bush Administration lied. This is now officially known. But it goes on fooling people with the reasons for its new crusade. In a fascinating report produced by the Strategic Studies Institute of the US Army War College, carried by the French daily *Le Figaro*, Dr Jeffrey Record notes:

> The invasion of Iraq was a strategic mistake ... This needless preemptive war was a distraction from the more necessary one against Al Qaida. It is counter-productive because it diverted the required resources for safeguarding American territory against terrorism ... Operation Iraqi Freedom has increased the terrorist threat ... The war was a big strategic mistake because the administration did not take into account the major differences between Al Qaida and Iraq.

As for the US army, he says: "It is now reaching its breaking point." He recommends a continued pursuit of Osama bin Laden and other Al Qaida members and internationalisation of US forces in Iraq through a legitimisation process involving the UN as a major player.

The latest polls, which show Bush far ahead of his challengers in the US presidential race, will not make this administration change anything, and Bush will continue to emphasise some of the facts while covering up others. Saddam's capture will be hailed, and the increase in the level of alert, both in Iraq and elsewhere, downsized. The "success" of the American policy in Iraq will be highlighted, but its dependence on Shia clerics not. "Freedom in the Middle East" will cover up for Guantanamo. "We launched a war against a country which was not an immediate threat for the security of our country," former Secretary of State Madeleine Albright wrote recently. Meanwhile, the US budget situation is becoming explosive even though it will be some months before the people discover this. The road is thus cleared for other kinds of manipulations, such as the decision to allow Canada to bid for Iraqi reconstruction contracts, even though the country opposed the war. No one took the trouble to point out that the latest "Engineering NR List" of the world's top international contractors puts the first Canadian construction company in 86th position, leaving room for the Bechtel and Halliburton construction companies, whereas five of the ten top-ranked companies are German or French.

Actually, only dedicated American zealots such as Amir Taheri still spend time criticising the arguments put forward by those who rejected the US war against Iraq. In this respect, it is by far more instructive to read what William Kristol, the neo-conservative editor of America's *Weekly Standard*, said in a recent interview with the French *Politique Internationale* magazine:

> Maybe the danger was not that imminent, but we cannot any more allow ourselves to make a distinction between a theoretical threat and immediate threat. The American government avoided divulging its true motives behind the intervention in Iraq in order to bring about a democratic political system in that country. They hope this will constitute both a model for the region and a pole of stability in a growing volatile environment.

In other words, "You did not do anything wrong but you could have" and "We are the ones to tell you what is good for you." Just after announcing that the US were going back to space, there is no reason why this president would not go on driving us up to the moon.

HEADSCARF SCARE CREATES A NEW LAW IN FRANCE

2 February 2004

It started off with two French teenage sisters, born to a non-practising Jewish father and a non-practising Muslim mother. Since they lived in one of those areas where integration is an everyday challenge, they found a way of getting themselves noticed – wearing a Muslim headscarf to school, something that is not really part of French tradition. In normal circumstances, any school headmaster would have warned the sisters and sent them back home if they refused to dress like other students. Unfortunately in France, when one lacks authority, one writes a law.

Two years and about 200 cases later (out of the five million Muslims in France), the French parliament is about to pass a bill which, thanks to an awkward coalition of Anglo-Saxon and fundamentalist opponents, is causing unjustified concern in the Arab world. The law basically says one thing: wearing a religious symbol, such as a Muslim headscarf, a Christian cross or a Jewish yarmulke is not forbidden, but wearing it in an ostentatious way in a state-run institution is. In other words, people attending a state-run school or working in public administration should not make their religion known. This is because in France, a country where there is no "official religion", many people of various faiths live together. When it comes to attending lectures or obtaining any kind of forms from the civil servants, it is neither necessary nor desired for either the recipients or the civil servants to show which religion they belong to.

For a clearer understanding, the whole issue has to be seen in the context of French history. After the downfall of the Roman Empire, the Catholic Church took its place and progressively extended both a temporal and a spiritual influence over Europe. In the past thousand years, France has witnessed a struggle by the central power against both the Church, which was interfering in every aspect of social and political life, and nobility, which did not want to abide by rules imposed by a centralised power. This fight was led by kings and emperors until the

19th century and then by the Republic. The issue of religion was only settled in 1905, with the so-called "Separation of State and Church" law. This law was seen as a terrible blow to the Catholic Church and, as normally happens in such circumstances, it also led to excesses. The Pope considered himself a "prisoner" in the Vatican City at that time, a situation which prevailed until the Church finally recognised that its power was essentially spiritual. Looking back, the 1905 law was intended to facilitate co-existence between different religions, and its latest achievement was the recent setting up of an organisation called the French Muslim Council. For the first time in history, an organisation would represent Muslims' views to the French government. This is more or less similar to what had happened with other religions.

Yet was it necessary for the headscarf issue to be settled by passing a law? What initially appeared to be a problem of simple authority at school led the way to a passionate debate about religious freedom, notably fed by Muslim extremists and advocates of strict secularism. The whole issue being more a matter of authority than of a headscarf, one wonders whether a law will solve anything or whether the state may be the right authority to define what a religious sign is or is not. But France is a country where the dates for the start of the hunting session are passed in parliament. And this "Franco-French" debate is the kind of issue the French love to discuss, despite Montesquieu having said: "Useless laws make necessary laws weaker."

The main issue here is not the relationship between Islam and society. It is more about assimilation. Francis Fukuyama of the Johns Hopkins Centre recently wrote:

> French citizenship is not based on ethnicity but is universal. The republican tradition recognises only the rights of individuals, not groups, and its commitment to secularism remains strong. The ultimate goal of the policy is not to crush religious freedom but to promote assimilation.

That is why the French foreign minister took the opportunity to return to the issue during his recent visit to the Middle East. His message was very clear:

> Islam has, of course, its full place in France and is respected there and indeed, it is to ensure respect for religions and beliefs that the

state has to be neutral. This is the French tradition of secularism, designed to promote integration and equal opportunity, which in France requires neutrality in public affairs.

Finally, this debate may not prove to be entirely useless, if it helps to reflect the image our western society conveys of women in today's world, or the respect everybody should have for local culture and traditions – for instance, the way one could better integrate immigrants who are given nationality, precisely because they are prepared to share common values and mutual respect.

"UPON THE WALL, I WRITE YOUR NAME, FREEDOM"

16 FEBRUARY 2004

Fifteen years ago, the Berlin Wall collapsed under the weight of a people's desire to be free. And now, in 2004, Israeli Prime Minister Ariel Sharon carries on with the construction of another wall of shame. A common characteristic of liars is their constant ability to distort the facts. The erection of an eight-metre-high concrete wall on Palestinian land is the latest travesty of the truth. There is nothing new about this, but as long as life goes on, no sensible human being should stop opposing it. Whatever you call it – a "protective fence" or an "anti-terrorist barrier" – a wall is a wall, and the fact that it may not be eight metres high throughout or may be painted with bright colours, changes little. A wall divides a continuous entity. If that entity is your property, it just splits into two parts, with your fields or your cattle on one side and your house on the other; if that entity is your country, you are separated from your work, your family, a hospital, a school … Is it necessary to describe the kind of despair a population held hostage may suffer from such a violent, although apparently static, action? Avraham Shalom, a former chief of the Israeli internal security agency Shin Beth, wrote:

> To make a wall a good thing, both parties should agree on it. Nobody will believe us if we limit ourselves to saying that the only reason for the wall is fighting terrorism. If that had been the case, it would have followed the 1967 Green Line. Security cannot exist if it is not accompanied by a political opening.

But Sharon goes on hushing people like cattle in a cowshed and putting free human beings behind the bars of a concrete jail. "Hostage", "ghettos", words that humankind hoped had disappeared, spring to mind. Does a violated child have to violate? And forget what was done to him?

The wall is morally repugnant because it opposes the natural principle of people living together. The rest is insignificant. Who would argue about the legality of genocide or discuss the efficiency of torture, if one admits that torture is morally unacceptable? Pope John Paul II recently told Palestinian Prime Minister Ahmed Qorei: "What the Holy Land needs is reconciliation; forgiveness and not revenge; bridges and not walls." Even though the International Court of Justice (ICJ) would rule that the wall is illegal, Sharon won't budge. He will rest peacefully, unless the present corruption charges against him keep him awake. He wouldn't bother about another useless resolution from the United Nations General Assembly since, as everybody knows, only resolutions against Iraq have a chance of being enforced.

The wall, however, fits within a more global policy: "The barrier he [Sharon] is building between Israel and the West Bank is closely linked to his Gaza withdrawal plan," writes the *Wall Street Journal*, to whose conventional wisdom, "it is not occupation that drives terrorism but terrorism that keeps occupation alive". Before asking who will erect the wall that will protect Palestinians from the regular incursions by the Israeli army into their cities, one has to realise that Sharon has been trying from the very beginning to get rid of the "silly" roadmap, which contemplates the existence of two states: a viable Palestinian state, living side by side with Israel. As far as he is concerned, any Palestinian entity, be it a "state", a "Palestinian authority" or a "bantustan" will never ever be allowed by Israel to rule itself on a territory larger than about 45 per cent of the present West Bank. The main challenge is to prevent the US from intervening in the matter. As the presidential campaign is currently underway in the US, there should be nothing to fear. (Presidential candidate Bush did not even mention the words "Palestine" or "Israel" in his State of the Union speech two weeks ago.) What is done is done, and any advantage gained on the field has better chances of surviving. Sharon, who recommended the building of several Jewish colonies that would divide the Gaza Strip, has long believed that "Netzarin was the same as Tel Aviv" and therefore, "evacuating Netzarin will only encourage terrorism and increase pressure on us". So why is he leaving now in a "land-for-nothing" move if not because the wall is killing any chance of progress towards a two-states solution? A unilateral decision to evacuate this land, remove some illegal colonies (which remains to be seen) and withdraw within a territory – significantly extended, thanks to the wall – may be accepted later on by the US, whoever the new president is. Of course, this looks like bargaining and this is probably why it is so shocking, because the matter of the bargain is human lives – not

Jewish of course, but still human lives. Some local Arabs, having carefully been kept within underdeveloped economic conditions, will thus be retained, in order to provide cheap labour for the new masters. The Arab world will go on crying in the streets and some politicians will take the subsidies that European governments will go on paying in order to keep their own consciences clear.

This is why the construction of the wall must be stopped. How many Israelis will have to die and how long will young Palestinians have no other choice in life than to die for their homeland? How long will the continuing Israeli violence forbid them from living in their own country? "It would have been hard, in the aftermath of World War II, to imagine that the state of Israel, whose creation was intended by its Zionist founders as a cure for the malignancy of anti-Semitism, would itself be seen as being the heart of this disease's recrudescence. Preventing injustice should hold a higher priority for friends of Israel – and Israelis – than preventing exploitation of criticism of that injustice by anti-Semites," writes Henry Siegman in the *Financial Times*. "If Israel's policies are unjust, we should say so." We do, but who listens? Isn't it time to start getting rid of Sharon: let's judge him for what he did in Lebanon,[1] what he provoked when he took his stroll at the Dome of the Rock, and remind him that there is no more need to run, since there is no Nobel Prize for hatred. As for us, "Upon the crushed houses, Upon the wall of the shame, I write your name, Freedom …"

NOTES

1 During the Israeli invasion of Lebanon in 1982, the Israeli army reached Beirut in August. In retaliation to the assassination of Lebanese leader Béchir Gémayel, Israeli Minister of Defence Ariel Sharon let the Christian militia headed by Elie Hobeika attack the Palestinian refugee camps of Shabra and Shatila located in the southern suburbs of West Beirut. About 2000 civilians, including women and children, were killed on that occasion under the supervision of the Israeli army who did nothing to prevent it. This is where General Sharon's nickname "the butcher of Shabra and Shatila" comes from. Although he was not held directly responsible for the massacre, his indirect responsibility was recognised by an Israeli court and he was forced to resign. General Sharon was sued by survivors in a Belgium court in 2001.

ONE MAY PREFER DEMOCRATS TO SMOKING GUNS

1 March 2004

A "New Vision for a Greater Middle East" has become the talk of the day. A G8 summit to be held next June at Sea Island will address the issue, to be followed by another one in Istanbul under the auspices of NATO. Basically, the vision involves promoting democracy in the Arab world – Pakistan, Afghanistan, Iran, Turkey – and Israel, "the only 'democracy' in the world where discrimination is institutionalised; where it is not a problem but a policy", according to the Arab League's former Ambassador to the UN, Clovis Maksoud. The scope of the new vision also includes economic reforms, so that these countries may be able to face the demands of their fast-growing population (6 million new jobs have to be created every year to meet the needs). Arab countries would thus be required to adopt political reforms aimed at "respecting human rights" – namely, enhancing the role of women in society – as compensation for what western countries would be prepared to do – increase financial help, facilitate entry to the World Trade Organization (WTO), support the creation of financial specialised institutions aimed at promoting the private sector or favouring the emergence of small- and medium-size enterprises. Regional developmental institutions similar to the European Reconstruction and Development Bank (ERDB) could collect funds from the region's wealthiest nations to help finance education, health and basic infrastructure.

The war in Iraq should, in that respect, be seen as an example: as United States Deputy Defence Secretary Paul Wolfowitz acknowledged, the war was not because of any immediate threat that Iraq represented to the US. It was the first step in a far wider strategy aimed at reshaping the Middle East, pushing for regime changes to agree to American conditions (the fight against terrorism and denouncing weapons of mass destruction). A next step is to move towards other well-identified targets: Syria, Iran and tomorrow North Korea. During the course of a presidential election year, it is enough that Iran keeps quiet (for good measure, Israeli Chief of Staff General Saül Mofaz warned of a possible pre-emptive strike on Iranian nuclear plants), whereas Libya helping the US strategy is welcome. Apart from the fact that Arab public opinion will never buy the idea, the true failure of this vision can be gauged from three main sources.

First, is the frightening example of the war in Iraq. Putting aside the official reasons for the war (all of which proved to be false), an honest analysis of the day-to-day events in Iraq or in Afghanistan highlights a basic failure: that of the "what is good for you is what we think is good for you" policy. This is why countries that opposed the war but nevertheless are ready to bring help to Iraq or Afghanistan, want to make absolutely sure that they talk to genuine representatives of these people, and not to puppets manipulated by foreign hands. "Many Iraqis have insisted on the fact that only an elected government could sign any bilateral security agreement with the Coalition and that any other alternative would be illegitimate," concludes the report prepared by the UN further to its recent mission in Iraq. This is a far cry from November 2003, when US proconsul in Iraq Paul Bremer was telling the interim government that it had "two hours" to accept the then proposed agreement. Despite the satisfaction of seeing the end of a brutal dictator, the question that arises now is how to move forward without the consent of the population and the support of the world's largest association of countries, the UN.

Second, any vision of the "new" Middle East cannot point exclusively at security matters, for "stabilising the Middle East" is obviously not enough to just get rid of terrorism. Do we live in a safer environment today than the one prevailing a year ago?

Third, there is a real problem of methodology. As French Foreign Minister Dominique de Villepin recently said in an interview: "It is our conviction that our starting point should be meeting the needs and expectations of the countries of the Middle East and not to try to impose our own views on it", something recently echoed by President Mohamed Hosni Mubarak while rejecting any "ready-made" solutions. "It is essential to associate the countries involved with our own thoughts as much as possible, in the logic of a true partnership. One should avoid too uniformed an approach; countries in the Middle East are different; our approach should be global and take into consideration all political, economical, social, cultural and educational aspects," Villepin said. To sum up a vision which is in such sharp contrast to the unilateralist one of the neo-conservative Bush Administration, Villepin designates the areas of mutual discussion: "First, there should be political dialogue in order to make democracy, good governance and human rights move forward; second, there has to be economic and social development so as to implement the necessary structural reforms; finally, supporting civil society in order to facilitate a dialogue between the cultures." Any other approach would undoubtedly lead to a confrontation between the western and Arab world.

But the main reason for an anticipated failure of the "new vision" for the Middle East is the unconditional support which the US have always given to Israel in its war against the Palestinians. "If we want to have some credibility, we cannot ignore the Israeli–Palestinian conflict. To create a peace dynamic is an unavoidable condition to any initiative in the Region," said Villepin in his interview. This is also the conclusion of Maksoud in a symposium held at the Paris Arab World Institute 4–5 May 2004 recently: "Whatever the deficiencies in the Arab world, nothing will happen until a fair solution is found to the Israeli–Palestinian conflict. This is the key to everything."

The vision for the Middle East must include a global approach, a true partnership and a peace dynamic through the settlement of the Israeli–Palestinian conflict.

BUSH HAS NOT ACHIEVED HIS JOB

15 MARCH 2004

President George W. Bush said recently: "Who can deny that we now live in a safer world?" I do. Not only do I deny it but I also accuse and blame President Bush for not having achieved the job. Despite there being unanimous international support for the war in Afghanistan, today no Afghan member of government can leave Kabul at night without putting their life in danger – because the US army there, and elsewhere, was distracted from what should have been its main goal, the fight against terrorism. The US army was given other goals and, as a first step, "bringing democracy to the whole Arab world". US forces were diverted to Iraq, from which there was no imminent threat of war, where no weapons of mass destruction could be found and no link at that time with Al Qaida could be established. For sure, the ideological crusade of the Bush Administration led to the ousting of Saddam Hussein. But that could have been achieved through other means, notably internationally approved intervention. Besides, the main issues were left unresolved. This is why Bush's handling of the "war against terrorism" will become a key issue in an election year. How many tragedies like the one that occurred in Spain last week (where terrorist bombings resulted in several deaths) have to happen before the Bush Administration understands that nobody can fight terrorism alone? What happened in Spain can happen in another country tomorrow, because nobody is immune. How long will it take before the Americans realise that they cannot live in "a safer world" because they are protected by the Atlantic? Similarly, others believe that they are safer when under the protection of their six-metre-high concrete wall.

A "global war against terrorism" cannot be led on the assumption that whoever plants a bomb is a terrorist. During the Second World War, many resisting nationalists killed people with bombs. Occupying Nazi troops used to call them "terrorists", just as the British used to refer to Ben Gurion, Menachem Begin and their friends as "Zionist terrorists".

Now they are heroes. There are no "good" terrorists or "bad" terrorists, but putting everyone together is not very smart either. Equating those who killed 201 innocent people in bombings in Spain with the Palestinian bus driver, a father of five, who blew himself up in a gesture of absolute despair at an Israeli army check-point located on his occupied land will not help fight terrorism efficiently. Every day, the situation is worsening in Occupied Palestine. There are daily Israeli army incursions into Palestinian land, continued violence and humiliation, destruction of houses by bulldozers as in Rafah (a UN report mentions that 1075 houses or buildings have been destroyed since October 2000, leading to 289 deaths, among them 79 children), the unabated erection of a concrete wall and targeted killings followed by suicide attacks.

Is that a valuable result of a foreign policy? Yet, how could it be otherwise when one reads what American Deputy Secretary of State Richard Armitage said in a terrifying interview in *Gulf News* on 1 March: the wall is no more a problem because "the security barrier has changed its route and has shortened"; security matters will be solved the day "Chairman Arafat, someone we cannot deal with, will hand over security to the Prime Minister"; Arafat "had years and years to reach decisions". Armitage should realise Bush and Israeli Prime Minister Ariel Sharon never answered Saudi Crown Prince Abdullah's proposals in the 2002 Beirut Summit to offer Israel a comprehensive peace if it would withdraw to the pre-1967 borders. The Israeli army can steal US$10 million from Arab banks "that was intended to fight terrorism" with total immunity provided. Who will believe that President Bush "made the right decision in Iraq after successive UN Security Council resolutions were ignored", when Israel bluntly rejected the numerous resolutions passed against it over the years? What kind of law is it which says that "the burden of proof rested on Saddam Hussein, not on the UN" before deciding to invade the country. Did, for instance, the Spanish people who died in the Madrid bombings have to prove that they were innocent before being struck?

Some analysts equate all criticism of American policies with anti-Americanism. One knows that nothing positive will emerge in the region until the US presidential campaign is over in November 2004, although when listening to Armitage, one may rightly wonder whether this makes any difference or not. Candidate Bush will spend millions of dollars showing his face on TV screens and terrorism will continue despite American neo-conservatives giving lectures on how to make a safer world. Unfortunately, they will have missed two major issues: nobody can fight terrorism alone, and ignoring the Israeli–Palestinian conflict will only lead to further chaos.

SHARON WILL CONTINUE TO ATTACK

9 April 2004

"In the long run, the elimination of Sheikh Yassin may have been a tremendous step towards peace." This is what the *Wall Street Journal* wrote on 23 March 2004 after the assassination of the spiritual leader of Hamas. Though much has been said about the assassination, it is necessary that we return to it, as the whole environment has now changed. In a long, hate-filled article that was indifferent and insulting towards the Palestinian people, the *Wall Street Journal* – why not simply call it the *Wall Journal* – stood by Israeli Prime Minister Ariel Sharon. It defended what the rest of the world – with the exception of the United States – condemned as an extra-judicial killing. "Not only are extra-judicial killings contrary to international law, they undermine the concept of the rule of law which is a key element in the fight against terrorism", European Union foreign ministers declared. "An extremely stupid action universally condemned, but by the US, this killing is a big escalation in the conflict which in addition will spill over into the international arena," said Britain's *Financial Times*, March 2004. It concluded by saying: "The assassination campaign will encourage terror, not counter it." Palestinian Prime Minister Ahmed Qorei described the assassination as "a crazy and very dangerous act". He added: "Yassin was known for his moderation and he was controlling Hamas." The *Wall Street Journal* doesn't care because, for it, "in order to succeed, Israel must be able to deny Hamas the ability to claim victory for the withdrawal [from the Gaza Strip]. Otherwise, it would raise Hamas's standing among ordinary Palestinians", and its cover page led the way: "Targeting of leaders signals plan to unilaterally define future Palestinian state". But the choice is not between full success or total destruction and Sharon is doubly wrong: first, because the withdrawal issue is different from the question of knowing who will hold the reins in the "liberated" Gaza Strip; second, because contrary to what Israeli Army Chief of Staff Moshe Yaalon declared, the assassination of Sheikh Yassin will do little to harm Hamas in that part of Occupied

Palestine. As long as Hamas is able to collect and distribute millions of dollars worth of aid to the Palestinian people – it has distributed US$200 million in aid since the start of the Intifada – it may be worth trying to consider the group as an unavoidable interlocutor.

Yet this tragic event should also be seen through the spectrum of other related issues. One of them concerns the position of the Bush Administration. White House Spokesman Scott McCleffan declared: "We are deeply troubled by this morning's action in Gaza." An assassination carried out by the Israelis using US-provided aircraft is an "action", but committed by Palestinians it is an "act of terrorism". Besides, the Bush Administration is only "troubled". One must wonder what would have to take place in order for it to be appalled. The crucial point is that, as the *Financial Times* put it: "The US alone has real influence with Israel. But it has forfeited its credibility in the Arab world because of its willingness to endorse almost anything Israel does." However, the US cares little and Arab money continues to flow in their country. A few Arab governments have indeed been accused of mouthing their disapproval while continuing diplomatic business with Israel. Hearts are bleeding in Palestine, but it is business as usual elsewhere.

Another issue concerns the way Israel is increasingly perceived outside of the region, notably in Europe. "Israel lost nearly all its friends," writes staunch ally Alexandre Adler in the French daily *Le Figaro*, although he stops short of explaining why. The *Wall Street Journal* considers that "the beginning of the current round of conflict can be accurately traced back to January 2001 when Yasser Arafat rejected the Clinton/Barak offer". The truth, though, is very different: Israel began losing many friends after the 1967 war when, despite two UN resolutions, it started defying international law, occupying lands illegally, and sending civilians into refugees camps and jails. Sharon and his friends in the Likud believe that they have been smart enough to portray any opposition to their criminal policies as a condemnation of Israel itself. Many analysts, including the most professional researchers, have had to defend themselves these past few years against the infamous accusation of anti-Semitism simply because they dared to oppose Sharon's policy. Pascal Boniface, director of the Institute for International and Strategic Relations (IRIS), has written a fascinating book entitled *Are We Allowed to Criticise Israel?* The conclusions are alarming for all those who love freedom. It seems that the "exceptionalism" of the ultra-Zionist community should be accepted as a whole without any discussion. This is precisely the kind of behaviour that feeds anti-Semitism. An Israeli writer, Erfal Sivan, said that "by qualifying non ultra-Zionist positions as 'anti-Semitic', the French Jewish community institutions become themselves a vector of violence". A former Israeli Ambassador to France said of the community, before leaving France: "If I am worried, it is because I have been able to assess the radical deviance which threatens your community." Yet, Sharon and his friends will continue their attacks against whoever doesn't share their views, especially in France where it is essential to them that the country be sidelined in order to prevent it from playing any role in the Middle East. Even though everything that had to be said about Sharon was actually said, why should one keep quiet about the continued use of force as the only instrument of policy in the face of daily humiliations, torture and deaths? At this point, one could only agree with a former French Jewish community leader who urged his French compatriots "not to criticise the Jews for what they are but for what they do". No more, no less.

TAKING THE WRONG APPROACH TOWARDS DEMOCRACY

13 April 2004

To be right is of little comfort in the face of tragedies. This is what flamboyant former French Foreign Minister Dominique de Villepin may be thinking these days when listening to the news emanating from Iraq. Iraq is not yet a disaster but it is surely an ongoing tragedy: insurrection, dozens of coalition soldiers killed, civilian contractors murdered and their bodies mutilated, and foreigners being taken hostage (indicating a growing "Lebanisation" of the conflict). The West now has to ponder who, between Ayatollah Al Sistani and Moqtada Al Sadr, is best suited for Iraq. Is it indeed up to the western world to decide what should happen in that country? And is it the US army's mission to favour Al Sistani over Al Sadr, or the Shiites over the Sunnis or Kurds?

The Bush Administration's official reasons for invading Iraq were the country's alleged weapons of mass destruction and its links to Al Qaida. Neither has been proved to be the case. But the real reason was to eliminate the "centre of gravity of instability" in Iraq and remake the Middle East so that terrorism no longer has places to flourish. What happened is the exact opposite: terrorism has flourished in Iraq since the war as it never has in the past. And the decision to invade Iraq in the name of the war on terrorism "handed the enemy precisely what it wanted and needed – proof that America was at war with Islam", wrote former United States counter-terrorism czar Richard Clarke in his book *Against All Enemies: Inside America's War on Terror*. After the recent uprising in Nasseriyah, where Italian troops shot dead another dozen Iraqis, Italian Foreign Minister Rocco Buttiglione gave another example of the consistent lack of understanding that Bush's friends display: "The choice facing us is whether to abandon Iraq in the hands of Islamic fundamentalism or to contribute to the birth of democracy in the heart of the Arab world." But can anyone impose democracy? Even Chairman of the Defence Policy Board Richard Perle says no. To start with, let us be sure of what we are talking about: the Bush Administration decided that Saddam Hussein was not the right choice for the Iraqi people (which is understandable) and toppled him (which could have been achieved differently). It then decided that Ahmed Chalabi and his friends were best suited to run the country, but backed off when faced with local opposition. Therefore, it set up an authority with no powers and ran the country by itself. Now it is going to hand over authority to another non-elected body, but still doesn't know how to do it. "Mr Bush reiterated his support for the June 30 transfer. But the timing is less important than the fact that the US still have no plans for what will happen on that date," wrote the *Wall Street Journal*. But this doesn't matter: "With elections put off for some months anyway, the default transfer plan will probably involve retaining the Iraqi Governing Council in some form. The coalition is better off doing this on its own and leaving the UN out of it." Britain's *Financial Times* gives some hope when it writes that "hard pounding alone will get the US nowhere in Iraq. Only a political approach will win." But Bush's friends continue unabated: "If warnings to Tehran from Washington don't impress them, perhaps some cruise missiles aimed at the Busher nuclear site will concentrate their minds." Leaving the Bush Administration to "implement democracy" the way it does means taking the risk of seeing it being rejected forever by the people. This is the new "B&B" mixture: Bin Laden and Bush creating the conditions for an unavoidable fight between Islam and the western world.

The problem with people who think and decide on others' behalf is that they often consider everyone other than themselves to be wrong. This is not democracy. This is the reason why the Bush Administration's vision for a "Greater Middle East" will fail miserably.

Besides fighting terrorism, the whole Iraqi mission was aimed at focusing all efforts on social and economic issues while excluding the Israeli–Palestinian conflict from the picture. Last week, European Union foreign ministers also put the emphasis on democratic reforms in the strategy for the Middle East "without having them held hostage to the Israeli–Palestinian conflict". Still, a major difference with the US plan is that this strategy takes account of the differences in, and requirements of, individual countries. Nobody should try to impose their own views on any of these countries. "Consulting with our partners is key," says a paper expected to be presented to the G8 summit to be held in June. And if progress on the Middle East conflict is not to be a precondition for constructing the urgent reform challenges facing the countries, "it will not be possible to build a common zone of peace, prosperity and progress unless a just and lasting settlement of the conflict is in place". The lack of prospects for peace will make it harder for reforms. This is true for Occupied Palestine as well as for Iraq: the belief that toppling Saddam Hussein would instantly lead the Iraqi people towards the US version of democracy has now proved to be an illusion and people don't generally have patience with illusions.

In the course of waiting for the Arab people to answer such challenges, let's bid farewell to the outgoing French Foreign Minister who is now the Minister for Internal Affairs after the latest government reshuffle. To many observers, Villepin will remain the one who dared to oppose the views of the mightiest power in the world; the one who received a standing ovation on 14 February 2003 at the UN because he simply said that nobody, not even the strongest country in the world, can solve everything alone and unilateralism is a no-exit path that leads to chaos. "People's identity doesn't accept being hurt by the strength of a foreign country"; what should be managed is "the rise of immaterial factors such as identity, religion and culture", he said. As with General Charles de Gaulle's famous speech in 1965 in Phnom Penh about the American war in Vietnam, Villepin may be accused of a similar sin by the Americans: having been ahead of others. His departure would have pleased the Bush Administration, whatever qualities his European-minded successor Michel Barnier has. But as President Jacques Chirac recently confirmed: "France doesn't appoint a foreign minister keeping in mind what another country may or may not wish. He is appointed in order to lead the foreign policy of the country and as far as this is concerned, the President of the Republic is the one in charge." Who would have doubted?

THE USE OF FORCE WILL LEAD TO NOWHERE

26 April 2004

Some countries believe it is enough to have an inept foreign policy and not be arrogant as well. The Bush Administration is proving one can have both. After the collapse of the Berlin Wall in 1989, the United States emerged as a new empire, a power that can dictate its views to the rest of the world, at least in the military field – especially to a divided Europe. International relations have since been characterised by one element: the use of force. Yet 9/11 proved that even the strongest country in the world is not immune to certain kinds of terrorism.

"There are three ways to influence others," writes Joseph Nye of Harward's Kennedy School of Government: "Threaten them with sticks, induce them with carrots, or entice them with values and culture. But 'soft power' – or the power to attract – would save a lot in blood and treasure. Soft power will be essential to attract the hearts and minds of the majority." This is exactly what the Bush Administration decided not to do, letting the ideological vision of its foreign policy develop freely. This is a policy of "a President exceedingly reliant on religious faith to guide his hand during conflicts," says Bob Woodward in his book *Plan of Attack*. Whatever the situation, this policy is marked by a continued and increasing use of pure and brute force which only escalates conflicts and worsens the aggression/repression cycle before ultimately churning out a burnt and deserted land.

In Occupied Palestine, the events of the past two weeks – the assassination of Hamas leader Dr Abdulaziz Rantissi and blind US support for Israeli Prime Minister Ariel Sharon's unilateralist policy – show that the use of force continues unabated. Despite being mired in a corruption case, Sharon is stronger than ever after his latest trip to Washington, and after the subsequent shift in US policy. He laughs at the lack of present retaliation as if the terrible experiences of the past are worth nothing. But Hamas is increasingly emerging as an unavoidable partner. Combined with the radicalisation of the Palestinian population, this may progressively spread the conflict to the whole region. What will happen the day Sharon hits "well-identified targets" in Syria, Jordan or Iran?

As for the war on terror, which was supposed to legitimise the war against Iraq, Woodward's book, coming after former US Treasury Secretary Paul O'Neil and former counter-terrorism advisor Richard Clarke's books, is further evidence that the Bush Administration had decided to attack Iraq long before 9/11. Secretary of State Colin Powell was sent to the UN even after diplomatic manoeuvring had stopped. And a much-needed US$700 million was likely to have been diverted from Afghanistan to Iraqi pre-war spending. Independent studies show that 550,000 to 600,000 troops are needed in Iraq to keep the country under control. This is out of reach.

Whatever the results, pursuing the war in Iraq the way the Bush Administration does – taking hostages, insurrections, 700 civilians slaughtered on the streets of Fallujah – will only lead to more US casualties. There is no possible military victory for those who do not have the support of the local population. And it's not the job of Charles Krauthammer to write in the *Washington Post* who are the good Iraqis and who are the bad ones. Using force only will lead nowhere in Iraq. Even Francis Fukuyama of the Johns Hopkins Centre writes: "Only elections, not the UN, not the Arab world, nor any coalition of foreign countries, can legitimate a new Iraqi government." One year, thousands of victims and billions of dollars on, the results of the Bush Administration's policy in Iraq are apparent.

What should the international community do, now that Bush has killed the Middle East roadmap and boosted Bin Laden in Iraq? It would really be short-sighted to justify any kind of timely help to the Bush Administration in Iraq, on the pretext that we westerners are "all in the same boat". We are not, precisely because we did not want to board that boat, a tool for destabilising a region and boosting terrorism, as experience has shown.

To start with, Europe must speak with a louder voice. Some complain about Europe's lack of common view and availability of alternative policy. This is not correct. The first point is for Britain "to realise that its capacity for influence is far larger on Europe than on the US", as writes analyst Pascal Boniface, considering that Britain's national interest should make it more European. This is especially true further to the uneven overall success the country has drawn from its presence in Basra. It is time to give a new dimension to a transatlantic relationship based on a fair deal between America's power and an enlarged European Union's requirements. It will not be long before the new Europe understands that the new threats are not from the East but from home. As for terrorism, an efficient war against it should continue through reinforced co-operation with all involved parties – the US, Europe and, of course, Arab countries. For sure, a new transatlantic vision should not be held hostage to the delirious plans of an Israeli war criminal. That is something to be considered by those who feel secure today in what they believe is an exclusive American-friendly protective environment. The new terrorist threats will spread everywhere. Like it or not, it is the Bush policy in the Middle East that is mainly responsible for it. Isn't it time, according to Woodward's book, to look elsewhere than at promises made by the Saudi Ambassador to the US Bandar Bin Sultan to "fine-tune oil prices" in order to help in Bush's re-election? The emerging situation in the world may now deserve some brainwashing.

THERE'S NEED TO PILOT US PLANE BEFORE IT CRASHES

10 MAY 2004

A genuine question calls for a clear answer. The Bush Administration seems to behave as if there were no more management, let alone leadership, at the helm of American foreign policy. Whatever the matter – the war in Iraq, the roadmap to peace in Occupied Palestine or the transatlantic relationship – indecision accompanies its contradictory statements. And, as America is the strongest country in the world, nobody can remain indifferent; especially when fundamental policy matters such as types of alliance are progressively put into question because of the course of events.

Much has been said about the abuse of Iraqi prisoners at the Abu Ghraib prison. Yet, two elements must be emphasised. First, the US lied. This should not come as a surprise; we all know that since President Bush decided to invade Iraq, this administration has constantly lied about the reasons for the war, the supposed threats, the course of events, and the human and financial cost. And now it has lied again. It said it was not aware, but actually it was. It probably tried to cover up the whole story, but failed. And if it lied about Abu Ghraib, who is to say it did not try to hide other cases? What will be discovered in Guantanamo the day an independent inquiry committee is authorised to have a look at the way in which the "enemy combatants", who have been stripped of all their rights, have been treated while imprisoned for months?

Another striking element is the lack of sincere apologies. On 5 May, Bush said he found the treatment of some Iraqi prisoners "abhorrent" but stopped short of apologising. No excuse, but the taking into account of evidence. On the following day, the *Wall Street Journal*'s headline was: "Bush still faces doubts of voters on economy". This gives additional clues to those still in doubt about Bush electors' primary concerns. This is probably the worst element of the whole story besides the abuse itself. For sure, all armies from all countries one day or another have to face situations regarding scandalous human rights issues. The American claim of good faith, saying that if it had been Saddam Hussein the photos would never have come out, is just another lecture on democracy aimed at third world countries. But a certain form of indifference linked to a political willingness to humiliate more than to torture will have irreversible effects in the longer run, especially if Rumsfeld's declarations about his "plain responsibility" go on to be counterbalanced by a simple "we are deeply sorry" of National Security Advisor Condoleezza Rice.

As everyone knows, this administration is particularly adverse to admitting its mistakes. Is it enough to make its present position on the Israeli–Palestinian conflict less understandable than ever? After his recent trip to Washington, Israeli Prime Minister Ariel Sharon could legitimately be satisfied with his outstanding achievements: a written commitment from Bush confirming his strategy for the Gaza Strip and, in a complete shift of US policy, the acknowledgement that the 1967 borders – which they now call the 1947 borders – were an "illusion", the "right of return" must be ruled out and "a certain number of Jewish settlements" have to be maintained on the West Bank. Brushing aside two key elements of the roadmap – the creation of a viable Palestinian State, and the commitment that any plan must be negotiated by both parties – President Bush put all his weight behind Sharon. Thus he destroyed any remaining hope of a negotiated settlement and, incidentally, gained a few additional badly needed votes for the November election. But last week, American officials declared that: "The roadmap had to be implemented by both sides; that they would not prejudge final status issues such as the return of Palestinian refugees to Israel or the future of the settlements in the Occupied West Bank." Whom to believe?

Finally, regarding the expected contents of a new transatlantic alliance, which is also a matter to look at together with the Bush Administration's projects for a Greater Middle East and the war in Iraq, further questions emerge. In an astonishing comment following Abu Ghraib's prisoners abuse scandal, US Secretary of State Colin Powell declared: "We will discuss with our Arab friends and see with them which insurances and comments they need in order to make them sure that the President did not abandon them." Does he really need that when newly appointed US Ambassador to Iraq John Negroponte declares about Iraq: "A vital role for the UN would not come at the expense of the United States influence or interest"? What Powell should be telling his "Arab friends" is hardly of any interest as, if we consider the way things are going, the US is not going to have many friends any longer. This is one of the worst results of the Bush "policy": how long will the so-called "moderate Arab states" be able to maintain such a relationship when their people go on witnessing events like those in Abu Ghraib? A feeble character who was elected with a narrow win, Bush thought he could use force to be seen as a war leader, a powerful president flying the flag of his own values to be instantly shared by the rest of the "free world". But force turned out to be terror.

An impressive list of 52 former British ambassadors and senior officials have written to Prime Minister Tony Blair to warn him and register their disgust at his alliance with Bush. American diplomats have followed suit. Robert Kagan, a member of the Carnegie Foundation for Peace, has just published a book titled *American Power and the Crisis of Legitimacy*. To sum it up:

> The US need a legitimacy to fight the world threats. Only Europe, because together with the US it remains the heart of a free democratic world, can give this. But Europe seems busier in trying to restrain the American giant than in attacking terrorists. And since it doesn't further look willing to develop its own strength, the overall result will be a decrease of the global power protecting the democratic world.

In spite of some means mentioned by Kagan, there is one that he hardly addresses: the need to share common views, notably about what is terrorism. It is not our responsibility to say who should pilot the US plane, but it may be ours to make it land before it crashes and engulfs the rest of the world in fire.

DAILY HORRORS MUST NOT STOP THE LOOKING FORWARD

24 MAY 2004

While events in Occupied Palestine and in Iraq repeat themselves day after day with nothing but steady progress towards horror, analysis tends to be limited to only the latest event. And this is how people start missing the point, as it is taking place when more than ever it is necessary to shed light on what is likely to happen next.

In Iraq or in Afghanistan, for instance, America is said to spend US$65 billion annually. I doubt this will last forever. There has been no change in the Bush Administration's policy there and the "transfer of sovereignty" will be a farce as long as President Bush or the US Ambassador designated to Iraq, John Negroponte, are shaping it. There are many indications that the US will leave sooner rather than later. A real transfer of sovereignty will mean that Bush is prepared to change his policy and return to the international community. But his present endorsement of UN envoy Lakhdar Brahimi does not look like lasting. Rumours are circulating that American and British officials are working on a pull-out plan, and one can easily guess that Italian Prime Minister Silvio Berlusconi will not oppose it. A successful overthrow of Saddam Hussein was followed by a series of unforgivable mistakes and failures. The abuse of Iraqi prisoners at the notorious Abu Ghraib prison has added to this. Bush has said he will keep his compatriots informed on the transfer process through weekly meetings in a move aimed at showing that he is open to dialogue. But this is for the gallery; the matter is over and everybody knows it. Even Chalabi is jumping off the US boat. In the end, after considering all the costs of the war, it will be concluded that other roads could have been taken.

In Occupied Palestine, the horror steadily continues, with no prospects or hope for improvement: there will only be more violence. Everybody knows to expect nothing from Ariel Sharon. An essential contributor to the infernal "action–retaliation" spiral, Sharon will go on at any cost. Events in Gaza were unanimously condemned by the international community, but Sharon doesn't care and will continue not to care while Bush continues to describe Israeli incursions as "troubling". Most would term them "war crimes".

A few wishful thinkers recently expressed satisfaction that the US did not veto the UN Security Council resolution passed against Israel. But, in reality, the US did so because it knew such a resolution was totally useless. To confirm that, consider this from the Israeli Ambassador to the UN, Dan Gillerman, who said: "We were not required to stop demolishing houses; we shall thus continue." Why, indeed, would they refrain, if all they are doing is only "troubling"? Especially when Bush goes on adding, as he did last week at a gathering of the America–Israeli Public Affairs Committee (AIPAC), a powerful Israeli lobby group, that: "The US is strongly committed, and I am strongly committed, to the security of Israel as a vibrant Jewish state … Israel, as a democracy, has every right to defend itself from terror." Has Israel to destroy houses with people inside to be "vibrant"? Does Israel's "every right to defend itself from terror" include shooting Palestinian civilians like rabbits when they try to escape? Israel, and now the US, are increasingly becoming the most hated nations in the world. Will the American voter understand that, and accept that their country was travelling along the same path as apartheid in South Africa? The Bush doctrine, as expressed by people like Deputy Defence Secretary Paul Wolfowitz and Chairman of the Defence Policy Board Richard Perle, is ruining the relationship between America and the Arab world, which is not good for anybody. Even Jordan's King Abdullah admitted it, after US Secretary of State Colin Powell failed to convince Arab leaders of its good intentions during the World Business Forum in Amman. True, the occupation of Palestine doesn't prevent some Arab countries from continuing with their business as usual, whatever the summit. Yet, the world's future cannot be left in Sharon's hands. The whole international order is at stake and "its fragile nature makes any doom laden scenario seem plausible", as Philip Stephens wrote in Britain's *Financial Times*. Stephens concluded by saying: "We stand at the edge of the cliff. Iraq is a disaster but the world's future looks worse."

Other elements should be looked at carefully in the coming months. For instance, how long will the word "terrorism" be used indiscriminately by the US as at present? "Terrorists are trying to stop Iraq's march to sovereignty and peace," said the US proconsul in Iraq, Paul Bremer. This is not correct. Terrorists who kill soldiers and civilians alike while trying to overthrow democracy by force cannot be compared to nationalists fighting for freedom from occupation. Means can be similar and people occasionally join forces – no foreigner has ever been arrested in Fallujah, though – but confusing terrorism with a fight against occupation is not only an intellectual fraud, it is a mistake.

Another element for consideration is the time factor. When the Bush Administration talks of bringing democracy quickly to the Middle East, it forgets that barely a hundred years ago, one could still buy a seat in the British Parliament or that as recently as 50 years ago women in France got voting rights. Reforms must come from within.

These things require some time to be implemented and it should be remembered that not all means are acceptable. Torture, blind retaliation or mass murder are not appropriate ways. One should never lose one's soul while fighting one's enemies, for the enemy would otherwise have already won. This is what Sharon is now doing in Occupied Palestine, destroying the bases upon which the State of Israel was built.

Finally, it is clear that events will be influenced by people's ability to take their future into their own hands. Bush has already said that "Iraq was not yet ready to govern itself". He also said that "the US would leave the country if required to do so", but swiftly added that "it was unlikely that this will happen". Bush should be reminded of a comment by British Member of Parliament Lord John Russell in the 1850s: "When asked whether a nation is ready for freedom, my answer is: has there ever been any man who'd be ready to be a despot?"

NARROW IS THE ROAD TO DEMOCRACY IN THE MIDDLE EAST

7 JUNE 2004

The lesson may be hard to learn but nobody can deny that what happened in Al Khobar two weeks ago was the price being paid by the Saudi authorities for a lack of political vision. Growing unrest in Saudi Arabia, as seen in these past months, may become a threat and is surely not helpful for the stability of the region. However, the picture may not be that dark; oil rigs do not burn, pipe lines are buried deep beneath the desert and oil transportation is handled through computerised control rooms hidden in concrete bunkers. A terrorist attack is not a regime change, and Al Qaida alone will not be able to overthrow the Saudi government – at least as long as it is not supported by a large chunk of the population. The sensational headlines in the European press expressing concerns about a destabilised Saudi Arabia may thus be just another example of over-reaction whenever oil is concerned.

Actually, beyond the dramatic events in Al Khobar there is something much more grave that occurred in Yanbu a few weeks earlier but which almost went unnoticed. This deserves attention from all democracy lovers: terrorists involved in the attack did not shoot at Americans or Britons; they shot at "westerners", at "non-Muslims". As some witnesses in Al Khobar put it: "They shot the non-Muslims and tended to spare the other ones." It is no longer important who supports Ariel Sharon's policies in Occupied Palestine or the American handling of Iraq, and who does not; it is the good versus the bad, "Muslims against Crusaders" and the willingness "to cleanse the Arabian Peninsula of all infidels, to beat off Crusaders and arrogant forces in order to free the Muslim land and enforce the Sharia". This is the politics of fanatic groups; it is the "clash of civilisations" which may only lead to other deeper conflicts if not addressed efficiently.

Assuming that democracy is the right of the people to decide what they want, it should be protected and promoted. But if the word itself has a universal content, it also has many forms. Basically, it is a right granted to any individual human being to benefit by a choice, and not an obligation, to think on their own, to join a group and be protected by it, still leaving a minority with the right to express peacefully any other choice. But if democracy is a set of techniques – freedom of speech, free elections – it is historically a result of an internal process and, therefore, there are many types of democracy in existence. It is thus impossible to say that there is one single form of democracy throughout the world.

This is especially true when a democracy is attacked, usually in two ways. First, through the willingness of some people to forbid anyone else to think differently from them. This brutal opposition normally emanates from fanatic groups, be they politically or religiously minded. Once they attain power, they install a kind of dictatorship until they are wiped out by local resistance or external factors – in the long run, as history shows, such situations never last. The second way is more subtle. It comes to give the word a definition that is so much marked by a specific environment that whoever lives in a different environment cannot reconcile himself with that definition. How, for instance, could an Iraqi be a "democrat" if the only representation of democracy they have seen is the way American troops behave in Iraq? When the Bush Administration does everything in the Middle East "in the name of democracy", there should be no surprise that this is rejected completely. In doing so, America is simply killing the idea of implementing democracy in the Middle East. It should be held responsible for that because it puts at risk any other attempt to implement reforms on a step-by-step basis. Indeed, democracy cannot be implemented from abroad or with guns.

This is where the link with the necessary fight against terrorism gains substance, for the definition of terrorism is not simple. "I call the deliberate assault of unarmed populations 'terrorism'. I call the armed resistance that opposes repressive forces while sparing civilians 'anti-terrorism'," wrote French essayist André Glucksmann in a recent article in the *Wall Street Journal*. However, he limited his words to the Chechen resistance. We would love to see him write in a similar way about the Palestinians' struggle. Indeed, it is difficult to distinguish between national resistance fighters and fanatics, especially when their means look similar. But, surely, some "external factors" explain terrorism and even more surely feed it. It is, for instance, a widely held view that Osama bin Laden cares little about the struggle of the Palestinian people; still, Ariel Sharon's policy in Occupied Palestine lends strong support to Al Qaida. In other words, Bush feeds Bin Laden, and vice versa. This is further confirmed when the US approach towards terrorism proves to be twice wrong: first, because the analysis of 9/11 was mistaken – the refusal to acknowledge any link between the terrorist attacks and America's blind support of Israel; second, because once they identified the "failed states", the neo-conservatives thought democracy could be imposed through military force.

This is why some past behaviour must be corrected and the necessary action aimed at undercutting elements supportive of terror be taken. The latest gathering of Arab Heads of State in Tunis on May 23 did not say anything else when some basic principles were stated: the need for a good governance and political reforms (deepening the base of democracy, respecting human rights, allowing freedom of speech and independence of justice, promoting women's role in public life), and a condemnation of any attacks aimed indiscriminately at civilians. It is time the Saudi authorities stopped being complacent about extremist groups. Much is being said these days about the D-Day celebrations and about the definition of a new transatlantic alliance. To make it concrete, which means including in it an Arab component, couldn't we start getting rid of the kind of unilateralism that has prevailed for the past year and accept such basic concepts as full sovereignty for Iraq and a fair peace in Occupied Palestine?

IS AMERICAN DEMOCRACY HEADING TOWARDS TYRANNY?

21 JUNE 2004

The Bush Administration has misled the American people. It has been lying repeatedly for the past two years. This may not seem like anything new to us but to the United States Congressional Commission investigating the 9/11 attacks, it was. The Commission has just concluded that there was no credible proof of any link between Osama bin Laden's Al Qaida network and deposed Iraqi president Saddam Hussein. There were failed "public justifications" for the war – the existence of weapons of mass destruction which were never found, and the false notion that the war was about freeing Iraqis and the Middle East from tyranny (the latest polls show that 92 per cent of Iraqis regard US troops as occupiers). More than 10,000 Iraqis were killed on false evidence. But this does not prevent President Bush from denying facts, just like former presidents Richard Nixon or Bill Clinton. In the home of law and order, an abrupt lie is often considered the only survival mechanism by politicians. However, when the mighty do not abide by the law, tyranny is never far away.

Iraqi Prime Minister Iyad Allawi gave an interesting example last week when he declared: "The transfer of Saddam Hussein and of the others will take place in two weeks." An involuntarily comic reaction came first from the coalition's spokesman Dan Senor: "We cannot remit Saddam Hussein to a non-sovereign government." More revealing stuff came from Bush, who said there was no way of setting a timetable. "Saddam Hussein will be remitted once it is deemed appropriate." This will be decided by Bush himself. Even after being transferred, Saddam will remain under US custody. How miserable Israeli Prime Minister Ariel Sharon appears! He had to appoint a personal friend, Menachem Mazuz, as an Attorney General to ensure that the corruption case against him was closed.

A more serious example of deviation from the law originated in a January 2002 memorandum written by White House legal advisor Alberto Gonzales. His recommendations were that the Taliban fighters captured in Afghanistan be excluded from the provisions of the Geneva Conventions and the 1996 American federal law on war crimes. This was actually a starting point of a mechanism leading ultimately to the abuses of Abu Ghraib and other disclosed – and undisclosed – acts of torture at various places. In August 2002, the *Wall Street Journal* reports, the CIA was able to obtain agreement that its agents won't be pursued within the framework of the "war on terror". The legal argument was signed by the American Justice Department's highest authority, legal advisor Jay Bybee. Torture should be limited to "acts of extreme nature", he wrote, and could notably be justified against the terrorists of Al Qaida. Any kind of "interrogation" could take place because the US interpretation "did not require sanctions for cruel, inhuman or degrading treatment". Nothing could then oppose a March 2003 Pentagon report attempting to find a legal basis for harsh treatment, even torture. The President could lead the war against terrorism "with all available means", whereas Defence Secretary Donald Rumsfeld himself was approving a list of 17 "questioning techniques" that were undoubtedly … questionable. To the question "Chain of command: can torture in Iraq be linked to the White House?", Britain's *Financial Times* answered last week as follows: "Abuses of Iraqi prisoners at Abu Ghraib may not have been isolated events perpetrated by low-level soldiers, but were the consequence of a systematic Bush Administration policy designed to extract information from reluctant detainees." The Bush Administration shows a constant disrespect of international law. Why have Guantanamo, if not because the US courts would probably have no jurisdiction over detainees held at the base? Why were the Geneva Conventions by-passed, if not to have a free hand as far as the handling of prisoners of war was concerned? Why the disdain for the new International Criminal Court, if not because American soldiers' immunity would no longer always be protected?

As Jeffrey Sachs of Columbia University recently wrote: "No society is immune from sliding towards Barbary, irrespective of its level of development." The abuses of Abu Ghraib show what happens when one decides to by-pass international laws such as the Geneva Conventions. The Bush Administration supporters – apart from the "kill-them-all" fanatics who still live in a world we hoped had disappeared – try to respond by explaining what torture is and what it is not. What happened in Abu Ghraib is "disgusting" but "does not include any element of torture", wrote the *Wall Street Journal* which considers that "stress positions are not torture either". What should we make of such definitions when Bush's neo-conservative friends praise the efficiency of Israeli's targeted assassinations of political leaders in Op-Ed columns? But even more worrying is the final word of the editorial, after it concludes that the rules of interrogation "deserve debate": "But we sure wish the moralising critics would keep in mind that this is also a debate over how to protect the United States"; that is, the belief that the United States could be protected "at any cost", and "with any means" (in other words, those which they are fighting with themselves). Meanwhile, Rumsfeld may decide not to enter the names of some prisoners or to transform "unlawful combatants" into "ghost detainees" who may occasionally disturb him at night. Indeed, tyranny is not far off when the winners show a disdain for the law.

WHAT IS SOVEREIGNTY WHEN THE US CONTROLS IRAQ

5 JULY 2004

By virtue of American democracy, a CIA-trained former Baathist with British connections has become the Prime Minister of a Shiite-majority country. After America's Italian and Polish allies enjoyed the ultimate joke by US President George W. Bush – who went ahead with the so-called "handover of sovereignty" without keeping them in the know – the question that arises now is whether the new government of Iyad Allawi will be able to re-establish security in a country ravaged by war and unrest.

Before that, let us put an end to a grotesque political farce that has been going on for far too long: "sovereignty". What sovereignty are we talking about? How sovereign is a country that is occupied by foreign military forces, which has no control over its air and sea ports, and which has no say in its internal security matters? "If I was the Iraqi general in charge, I'd be upset because there's a security company doing things I think I should be doing," said the Custerbattles security firm's representative in Iraq further to the announcement of contracts worth millions of dollars to British security companies. "US forces will stay in Iraq as long as it will be necessary and they will remain under the command of the Coalition," said Bush. But sovereignty is universal: it is not a transfer of some powers.

The United Nations unanimously came up with Resolution 1546 on 8 June. This resolution said that an interim government would fully assume power and take charge of the country, but will avoid any decisions that could interfere with the future of Iraq after the interim period. It also said that on 30 June the occupation will cease and Iraq will regain its full sovereignty. The alternatives originally conceived by the Bush Administration were either a Pentagon-supported Ahmed Chalabi with a radical regime change, or a CIA-supported Allawi with a mild de-Baathification process. This is where we stand now, but still America goes on pulling the strings. Each Iraqi "Minister", most of them having foreign travel and other documents, are seconded by American consultants. The

US "Embassy" has a staff of 1700, including 900 American citizens. Former President Saddam Hussein is "handed over" to the new authorities but still is "protected" by US forces. And his trial, which will (of course) be "fair" as it is in the hands of Chalabi's nephew, will take place on a US military base – provided he finds judges who don't get shot down once appointed. (Five have already been killed.) At least he will not have to look for local journalists: they are forbidden from attending. One should never forget that there is no example in history in which a country where foreign forces are present has enforced long-lasting political changes with success. An occupied country doesn't change its constitution. And if the Iraqis want to put their former president on trial, they should do it by themselves.

Hence it is no surprise that, given the present uncertain situation in Iraq, there is no consensus on the chances of success of the Allawi government. But as far as the Bush Administration is concerned, the odds are clear: it will lose in all cases. Indeed, the dilemma stems from the autonomy the Americans are prepared to give to Allawi. If they behave as they have done so far, violence will reach unprecedented levels and a "Vietnamisation" process will take root.

If, on the contrary, Allawi is given the necessary means to re-establish the rule of law, which goes beyond the presence of his US soldier-bodyguards, the return of law and order would obviously strengthen his position. But for this to happen, it is necessary that this former Baathist reverts to some methods or has recourse to some people that the Bush Administration and its Israeli friends do not want to be seen any more. This brings us back to the reasons for the war – reshaping the Middle East, bringing democracy and suppressing any threat to Israel. This cannot sit comfortably with the return of a strong Baath-minded Iraq. "There will be no return for the Baath and Saddam," Chalabi said in an interview. "My affiliation with the Baath party has given me a great political experience," noted Allawi. This is enough for the many Baathist cells spread over the country to resume activity, as they did with the creation of the United Council for Iraqi Resistance.

For now, the US will go on lying. The new American ambassador to Iraq, John Negroponte, whose track record on the death squads in Honduras[1] will re-emerge some day, will go on saying that the US has played no role in picking names or that in Iraq, American forces will be free to operate as they see fit. As a preliminary to Michael Moore's film

Fahrenheit 9/11, a documentary by William Karel, *The World according to Bush*, confirms that we have now entered an era of meddling, an end of national sovereignty and "the emergence of publicised emotions as a new guide for international relationship". In Iraq and elsewhere, America's partners have the choice of either aligning themselves unreservedly with Washington or being considered antagonists – "to be poodle or end up in the doghouse", as an analyst summed up recently. At a time when some European pro-Western politicians are calling for the re-building of a transatlantic alliance, one may rightfully wonder how this can happen when one has to talk with people who do not admit to controversy any more.

NOTES

1 More specifically, the "Iran-Contra scandal" is a mechanism set up by US officials in President Reagan's times to fund the activities of the Contra militias in Honduras (who were fighting in Nicaragua against a democratically elected government). Despite a clear injunction by the US Congress not to spend money for this action, illegal sales of arms to Iran were organised and the resulting funds used to finance the Contras. Elliot Abrams, now in charge of Middle East Affairs, was then responsible for US foreign policy in Latin America. John Negroponte (an ambassador to Iraq at the time of the writing) was an ambassador in Honduras from 1981 until 1985. He covered up human rights abuses (notably the ones committed by the US-trained Battalion 316) and the actions of death squads.

IF NOT ISRAEL, WHO MAKES THE WORLD MORE DANGEROUS?

19 JULY 2004

A year and a half ago, United States Secretary of State Colin Powell was indignant at the United Nations because the then government of Iraq would not respect the last two UN resolutions passed against it. "A story of disdain towards the international community represented by the UN," he said of an institution the Bush Administration was going to ignore shortly afterwards in an unprecedented move of arrogance vis-à-vis the rest of the world. But everybody also remembers that he was not taken seriously because the Israeli record of disrespect for resolutions passed against the country was even worse. Indeed, Israel cared little about resolutions, knowing that they would never be enforced against it. And no one can thus be surprised by Israeli Prime Minister Ariel Sharon's reaction to the recent non-binding judgement of the International Court of Justice (ICJ) on the Israeli wall that said that:

> The construction by Israel, the occupying power, of the barrier on Occupied Palestinian territory is illegal. It is a violation of the humanitarian international law because it restricts the freedom of moving of the Palestinians, preventing them from finding jobs, medical services or schools for their children. Israel is ordered to stop the construction of the wall in Occupied Palestinian territories and may even be asked to pay compensations for the damages caused.

Yet Israel will not abide, simply because this ruling does not suit it. "This decision is of no importance," said Sharon, "because it does not mention the existence of terrorism." To average people or states, the ruling of a judge normally applies in its entirety. But the "Chosen People" only accept what suits them. As a "unique" entity, how could Israel behave just like any other country in the world? Actually, nobody would have denied Sharon the right to build new ghettos, protected by six-metre-high concrete barriers, behind which his fellow Israelis could hide and live among themselves without any interference from outside – provided that this is built on their own land and not on Palestinian land which is temporarily occupied. This is what the ICJ said, because this is international law. But Sharon knows that the Bush Administration and its Zionist, neo-conservative friends will never enforce any resolution against Israel. Why, then, should he care about it?

Sharon was not even willing to give a hand to a friend – British Prime Minister Tony Blair – at the outset of the Iraqi situation. As everybody knows, there is one thing that can make Blair the happiest man on earth: the discovery of weapons of mass destruction in Iraq. But these could not be found, because they do not exist. In fact, Blair will likely be remembered by people as "Mr 45 minutes". It would have been so easy for Sharon to tell Blair where to find any such weapons in the region – something known for years in Israel. After 17,000 military personnel and civilians were killed, about 40,000 others wounded and US$150 billion spent for the wrong reasons, one could have expected some help from Tel Aviv. But the Sharon government will not confirm or deny the fact it has nuclear weapons. The director of the International Atomic Energy Agency (IAEA), Mohammad El Baradei, was in Israel two weeks ago. He hoped to meet with Mordechai Vanunu, the Israeli engineer who spent 18 years in jail because he was brave enough to mention the Israeli nuclear site at Dimona as the likely place to find between 200 to 400 nuclear warheads. The nuclear weapons here can be delivered using many of the American-provided delivery systems. (Does anyone remember the British uproar when it was revealed that some of the rockets owned by the former Iraqi regime could travel six miles further than previously thought?) Of course, Vanunu was not allowed to meet El Baradei. The Israeli government refused to recognise it had nuclear arms and it also refused to allow its sites to be visited because "Israel is forced to maintain … all the strength necessary for its defence", which is obviously not the case with the rest of the world, including Iran. Actually, international law clearly doesn't apply to Israel.

It is widely known that the group of American Zionists that managed to penetrate the US government after the last presidential election was waiting for an opportunity to impose its own agenda on the Middle East. 9/11 could not have come at a better time for them. Whatever the reasons for the attacks, and for sure none of them were good, it is difficult not to see a link between them and America's biased policies in Palestine. That may not have been in Osama bin Laden's mind, but it was surely in the minds of many in the Arab world when the event occurred. Israel and its friends projected the terrorist threat against the US as being Muslim and, subsequently, as an Arab threat against "the free world" – that is, a threat against Israel itself. "The Fourth World War could well be the war against militant Islam," says Norman Podhoretz, the neo-conservative editor of *Commentary* magazine in the US, whereas another neo-conservative, historian Bernard Lewis, adds about Muslims: "They have been hating us for centuries." "Us" refers to the whole world minus the Arabs. Once the Washington hawks start to endorse a vision of a world in which "evil" should be eradicated, what will happen if "evil" means the Arab world? A recent article about 9/11 in the *Washington Post* by yet another US neo-conservative, Charles Krauthammer, is symptomatic of this new line of thought. Islamic militants represent the new global threat the US will have to fight, he said, and as this is a product of the Islamic world, the "Arab world" for short, this is where the fight should be led. We have learnt to live with the delirious vision of these fanatic zealots for many years. But when this becomes the vision of the world's strongest military, one has good reasons to start worrying.

TURKEY'S ADMISSION TO EU IS A MATTER OF GRAVE CONCERN

2 AUGUST 2004

"The Turkish are very good people," said the Prince of Metternich 150 years ago after the Chio massacres in Greece. "They slaughter the Greeks and the Greeks behead them. It is a matter that has nothing to do with any kind of civilization." The question of Turkey joining the European Union (the first step of which may take 15 years to negotiate) is thus not a new issue. It officially started 40 years ago and was marked by a series of successive European Council rulings which never said no but led Turkey to believe that a yes would come with some unclear conditions. The latest one defined a precise deadline, December 2004, when it would be decided whether Turkey meets the so-called "Copenhagen criteria": respect for the state of law, democracy and human rights; and the achievement of a modernised economy able to address open competition. This is why political leaders began a frantic exchange in recent months about Turkey's history and civilisation, democracy, economy and international relations. The first concerns came from those who consider that Turkey is not part of Europe, neither geographically (95 per cent of its territory is in Asia) nor historically. The former Ottoman Empire in Europe was always linked to invasion, destruction and economic drawback such as in the Balkans or Cyprus. With its differing civilisation, its values would not be those upon which the EU was built. Turkey hit back at Europe arguing it should not be a "Christian Club" and should thus accept members of other religions (98 per cent of Turkey's 70 million population is Muslim). "Turkey is at the doorstep of Europe and wants to be part of the family," said Turkish Prime Minister Recep Erdogan. How could one dismiss a country that has been part of all the major treaties regarding Europe? What about the basilicas of Bezants, the colossus of Rhodes or the temples of Ephesus? "We see the EU as a union of political values. A place where civilisations can be harmonised and coexist in peace," added Erdogan, "not a place for a clashing of civilisations." Turkey would be a bridge between Asia and

Europe. For others, its heterogeneous population (including Kurdish tribes), the risk of jeopardising any balance in the EU and a refusal to recognise the Armenian genocide are enough to prove that Turkey is too far removed.

Regarding democracy, free elections, a neutral army and secularism, the progress achieved by the Erdogan government is amazing and its march towards democracy, including the status of women, should be emphasised. Much remains to be done, such as changing the attitude of over-zealous civil servants, enforcing application decrees for a judicial system that is still not protective (editors, for example, are imprisoned for holding particular opinions). So many reforms made so swiftly cannot be implemented overnight. And if the role of the Turkish army hardly goes with the view one has of a liberal democracy, it is agreed that it has behaved more positively than negatively in recent years. However, a sharp contrast occurs with regards religion versus secularism, and Turkey may not have played its hand very smartly. Once it had said that EU membership was crucial in bridging the divide between the West and Muslim worlds or to promote its future role as the only "Muslim democracy", it then resorted to a kind of blackmail in case the answer was negative: that there would follow civil unrest, the disappearance of moderate Muslims, expansion of Islamism. Excluding Turkey would be a terrible mistake in Muslim eyes. Yet, as long as five schoolgirls are allowed to drown in front of schoolmates who are not authorised to save them "because they would have to touch them", or the only training centre for Orthodox popes remains closed, there is still a long way to go. The concept of secularism means everybody is free to practise their religion or otherwise: this can hardly be respected when 98 per cent of the local clerics are on the state's payroll.

Economic arguments are not persuasive, even though the cost of living in Turkey is 25 per cent lower than in the EU. The risk of worker migration is remote when Turkey's low cost of living could result in new job opportunities (as with former Eastern bloc countries). The Turkish economy probably has more trumps than the figures show, and still 10 to 15 years to run before subsidies enjoyed by European farmers fully apply to it. The well-known deficiencies (notably high inflation) can be more than compensated for by a hard-working population (which will equal the German population in 2015), as well as prospects linked to oil transportation (via the Ceyhan pipe) and water availability.

Internationally, the debate was spoilt by American behaviour (this administration considering any savoir-faire a sign of weakness). Its overwhelming support of Turkey, when everybody knows about the good that Bush wishes Europe, was enough to raise doubts. Incidentally, it explains French President Jacques Chirac's comments: "The US would not want to hear France's views on its relations with Mexico." Turkey, the staunchest of allies of Israel, never maintained such friendly links with other Arab states. But the fact remains that Turkey has been an ally since 1952; its belonging to the EU would be a stabilising element in the region as well as a peace-strengthening one. And the need for the EU to reinforce its links with its other partners of the Mediterranean area surely does not oppose the joining of Turkey.

Considering such contradictions, it is not surprising that some rushed enthusiastically to German opposition leader Angela Merkel's proposal for a "privileged partnership", a way to maintain links with Turkey while avoiding the risk of its joining transforming the EU into an international organisation. The idea is bright but came too late because the EU has already become something that has little to do with what the founding members had hoped for. The original concept of Europe is now dead. What could not be achieved with 12 members with a strong Franco–German axis will not be achievable with 27 or 32 members, and the political vision in which cohesion is necessary for an efficient, powerful Europe with an autonomous strategy no longer exists. The only way to part from an open single market under the commending of the US is to start working on "reinforced co-operations" in some fields with those states that are prepared to move further ahead together. But for the time being, as Philip Stephens said in the *Financial Times*: "There are risks, of course, in giving Turkey its route map into modern Europe – serious ones. But the dangers of raising the drawbridge are infinitely greater." In the meantime, negotiations will continue to put pressure on Turkey to continue to reform.

WHAT'S A NEW TRANSATLANTIC ALLIANCE FOR?

16 AUGUST 2004

American troops are hardly pausing in their bombing campaigns in Iraq. The rest of the world cannot stop crying – without doing anything – about Israeli Prime Minister Ariel Sharon's hatred and violence in the Occupied Territories. And the transatlantic alliance rift is with us again. A common position these days among well-intentioned people on both sides of the Atlantic is that a new alliance should be built: the alliance, in the doldrums as a result of the Iraq war, should be restored. The present position of the alliance does not call for any further comments, with everyone following their own route. There are no more allies; only poodles or foes. If United States President George W. Bush needs to show American voters that he still enjoys support in Europe, his action, as recently demonstrated on a two-hour stop in Ireland, will be limited to a pre-written declaration that cares as much about European positions as the Halliburton does about open-market conditions. As for the rest – agriculture, aeronautics, defence industries or culture – Europe and the US seem to be at odds. The logical question, then, is whether shared values and remaining common interests outweigh the many points of difference. "The transatlantic divide must not be allowed to widen" say many analysts and politicians. Their solutions to put an end to the transatlantic rift are as follows.

On the American side, it could be time for a change of tune – for instance, not automatically regarding as an enemy anyone who is not in full agreement with Bush policy. America should also stop believing that it can run Iraq alone and try to be more balanced in the Israeli–Palestinian conflict. Finally, it could review its position on multilateral treaties, start restoring law (as it has *not* been doing in Guantanamo) and, ultimately, try to have about Islam and the Arab world a view that is not that of its Jewish community.

On the other side of the Atlantic, it could also be time for a change – especially with the French, whose anti-Americanism is tantamount to a national element of culture such as eating snails or frogs legs. Europe should also show it is prepared to lend a hand in rebuilding Iraq and put more forces into the international fight against terrorism, including the search for weapons of mass destruction. It should applaud Sharon's decision to evacuate the Gaza Strip. Finally, it should do everything it can to develop a strong European defence force aimed at eliminating the American burden within NATO.

However, all of this has little to do with the harsh realities of the international situation for at least three reasons.

The first is that the concept of an Atlantic alliance that everyone has known since 1945 died after the fall of the Berlin Wall in 1989 and remains to be defined further as a result of the 9/11 attacks. The intensive and fast-moving international flow of people and technology has also changed the horizon. The second reason is that an alliance is normally built against something or somebody. In the days of communism and the Soviet bloc, it was meaningful. But what about today? Even though limited solely to the fight against terrorism, it is no longer pertinent because no strategy can be limited to that. Which state would be ready today to sponsor terrorism officially? Furthermore, the sharing of similar values against terrorism goes far beyond the limits of an alliance between, say, America and Europe. It extends to nearly all the rest of the world. Third, it seems that the transatlantic alliance issue has now changed from "America–Europe" into "America–rest of the world". And the situation in this respect is not particularly bright for the US, at least according to a group of former US diplomats and military leaders who recently released a document saying that America has never been so isolated in the world and so feared. Besides Iraq, the Bush Administration's ineffectiveness in its approach to the world is also cited for the Israeli–Palestinian conflict. "The damage we've done to key and valuable alliances is going to take a long time to fix," said Ronald Spiers, a former US ambassador to Pakistan and Turkey. "What you now have is a collapse of trust," concluded Professor Shibley Telhami of the University of Maryland, further to recent polls commissioned by the Arab American Institute, which believes the war in Iraq will result in more chaos and more terrorism against the US and less democracy in the world.

This is why any new alliance in the future must first be defined between the partners. Yet how could it be when people like the American Foreign Relations Council chairman Richard Hass dare write that "it is not possible … that Europe defines itself as [an] equal or a competitor of the US", and that the only interest of Europe developing its military capacity is "to be able to intervene along [with] the US but not be comparable to the US"? The US is an obvious partner of Europe as a result of the shared values but, as French Foreign Minister Michel Barnier said recently: "The Atlantic alliance is no more a necessity; it has become a choice."

SHARON'S EXPANSIONISM CONTRAVENES INTERNATIONAL LAW

30 August 2004

As he runs frenetically against time, Israeli Prime Minister Ariel Sharon is giving the final touches to his Gaza evacuation plan. Basically, the plan involves giving back parts of the Occupied Territories where 7500 Israeli colonists live illegally (under the costly protection of the army) surrounded by 1.3 million Palestinians.[1] As compensation, the colonists are to be relocated in the West Bank where the present illegal colonies would be simultaneously ratified.

As Britain's *Financial Times* noted: "The Bush decision to give something between a green and an amber light to this new violation of international law is inflammatory and irresponsible." Yet despite this dramatic development, it seems many observers today have little to say about it, preferring instead to reflect on American policy in the Middle East over the years, or to engage with vague considerations about the personal future and survival of Ariel Sharon and Palestinian leader Yasser Arafat. They hold endless discussions about who should lead Israel or Palestine and often conclude that the conflict is beyond resolution if Arafat and Sharon remain in power. Indeed, Arafat would never make his promised reforms. The dysfunctional Palestinian political system would only have worsened over the years, and the emerging power struggle between inept and corrupt nationalist warlords and the leaders of the young nationalist guard would soon be exploding. On the other side, Sharon would not wish to see a strong and legitimate Palestinian leadership with a coherent strategy to secure a viable Palestinian homeland. "Sharon's intransigence has given Arafat his excuse while the Palestinian's obstinacy has provided the Israeli with his justification," writes Philip Stephens in the *Financial Times*. In another development, Dennis Ross, a former representative of the Clinton Administration to the Middle East, explains in *The Missing Peace* why Arafat should carry most of the blame. As he is now looking (along with his colleagues) for a possible reprise of their roles in any Kerry administration, the pro-Israel Ross forgets to look at the Palestinian point of view – the suffering caused as a result of the occupation and the doubling of the number of colonists. He doesn't even make any reference to the widening gap between the American Jewish zealots who are behind Bush's Middle East policy and the majority of Americans who oppose building new colonies. As a Ramallah-based researcher wrote, one may hope that any new American administration – if there is one – will look for deeper reasons for their failure in clinching a peace deal after the Camp David advances.

Regardless of the pertinence of these analyses, which may seem incongruous given the present situation in the Occupied Territories, preparations for an imminent drama continue unabated. Nobody will be surprised at Sharon's dedication to the Gaza evacuation plan. His plan could leave Israel in control of roughly half the occupied West Bank and therefore 90 per cent of mandate Palestine. Of course, the withdrawal from Gaza is not a prelude for Sharon to a Palestinian state, as people of good faith might think. It is an apparent and tactical retreat in order to annex larger chunks of Palestinian territories in the West Bank in pursuit of his ambition for a Greater Israel. Nor will anyone be surprised that his fellow Likud members oppose that plan and, at a recent party convention in Tel Aviv, won a non-binding majority for vetoing a national unity pact with Labour that could have offered an alternative majority in parliament. Likud extremists always had a very clear and straightforward solution to the Palestinian issue – send them all back to Jordan. But the amazing fact is the support Sharon has enjoyed from the Bush Administration. In April 2004, he persuaded Bush to endorse his plan's main lines. Last week, he moved one step further when it appeared that Bush would support his decision to construct 1000 new housing units in the West Bank. In 2003, the number of housing units in colonies rose by 35 per cent, while construction inside Israel decreased by 35 per cent. In 2004, colony construction projects will represent 12 per cent of the total construction work, whereas the colonists will represent 3.6 per cent of the total Israeli population. "We will study the file," said the Bush Administration in a first "threatening" move, until the *New York Times* disclosed that an agreement had been reached so as "to meet the natural growth of the population". During the Second World War, the Nazis also extended some detention camps as a result of "a growth of population". But the point is, they should never have erected such camps. The roadmap provided for a total freeze on constructions in colonies where 240,000 Israeli live. Bush himself has thus buried the roadmap, but it doesn't stop there. Under international law, all colonies in occupied land are illegal. The fourth Geneva Convention, which the Israeli Supreme Court has commanded Sharon's government to ratify, specifically forbids the occupiers from "transferring parts of its own civilian population into the territory it occupies". Sharon's expansionism contravenes international law, which is nothing new. But he undermines the moderate opinion of those who still believe in a negotiated solution. He will be held responsible for that, as for the rest.

Meanwhile, hiding behind a usual smoke screen, Sharon and his accomplices continue to entertain the world stage with gimmicks of their own. Last week, Israeli minister Sylvan Shalom was in France to ask it to change its laws "in order to better fight anti-Semitism". Actually, he was making a European tour in view of the forthcoming vote on the wall at the UN. "We consider that anti-Semitism and racism lead to terrorism. As we share the same democratic values, we should be united in the fight against terrorism, and fight the anti-Semitism and racism which feed it," he said. But we do not share the same "democratic" values of a country that doesn't respect international law, that treats its prisoners in an inhuman way and ultimately that refuses to acknowledge its own responsibility for terrorism.

Notes

1 The evacuation plan of the Gaza Strip is a unilateral decision by the Israeli government to pull out from Gaza, where about 8000 Israeli colonists live among 1,300,000 Palestinians (most of them in refugee camps) under heavy protection of the Israeli army. The plan was approved by the Israeli Knesset parliament, but only after Prime Minister Ariel Sharon formed a coalition government with members of the Labour party (his own party, the Likud, being split over the matter). The plan is a "unilateral" decision, and it means that the Palestinian authorities were not involved in the practical aspects of its implementation. Formally, the plan may appear as a first step towards the completion of the roadmap peace process by the Israeli side, according to which Israel should evacuate all the territories that it has occupied during the recent wars; it is also a positive signal given to US President George W. Bush. But on the basis of several declarations by Ariel Sharon and his advisor Dov Weisglass, it is also considered as a way for Israel to give up a piece of land of no strategic value (including the heavy cost incurred by the army who protects the colonists) and to take

advantage of this apparent good will in order to concentrate all its efforts on the Occupied West Bank: that is to say, to strengthen the existing colonies there, to annex eastern Jerusalem, reunify the city and make it the capital of Israel, and finally, to split the West Bank into two parts and prevent the possibility for the Palestinians to create a continuous state.

LEGACY OF A "WAR PRESIDENT" IS NOTHING TO BE PROUD OF

13 SEPTEMBER 2004

The American Presidential campaign still has a few weeks to run, and a few million dollars to be thrown around. Whoever wins the election – John Kerry or George W. Bush – and by whatever margin, America, as a powerful country, remains a compulsory reference point for the rest of the world. And that's why President Bush's staff will be interested in the latest multinational poll published by the US-based German Marshall Fund, three years after the 9/11 attacks. Beyond the information itself which, as is often the case, offers contrasting elements, one should look at the trend. Twenty-two per cent of the European countries polled thought a strong US role in world affairs was "very undesirable" in 2002. That figure is now 47 per cent. The majority of Europeans polled now oppose the US global leadership (55 per cent, against 31 per cent in 2002). More focused information refers to countries such as Poland or Turkey which, for years, were considered solid American allies. "The Turks are now more negative than even the French towards the US," writes the *Wall Street Journal*. As for Poland, where polls reflect frustration at sacrifices in Iraq or at the enforcement of the US visa programme, the situation is no better.

A consequence will likely be a new definition of the Atlantic charter. Yet, urgent issues such as terrorism need to be continuously addressed and the Bush legacy does not help in this respect. "Because of this administration," writes Joseph Biden, a senior Democrat on the American Senate Foreign Relations Committee, "America is less secure than it could be ... It is more alone in the world that at any time in recent history ... This President has thumbed his nose at the world and asked Americans to accept it as diplomacy." Surely, some of the past events in the US would illustrate a situation that the electors will be asked to sanction in November: the US$400 million Hollinger's scandal (where Richard Perle's name reappears), the Larry Franklin Israeli spy issue (which in other circumstances would have sent US Defence Secretary Donald

Rumsfeld to the floor), the rather disgusting activities of the Swift Boats Veterans for Peace association that Bush campaigners manipulated and, even more blatantly, uneven economic performances and a US$422 billion budget deficit. But a real issue in European eyes concerns the Middle East, and "the growing belief in Europe that the biggest threat to them is entanglement with the US in a misbegotten policy in the Middle East", as concludes the already cited Marshall Fund report.

When it comes to the Bush legacy in the Middle East, Iraq and Israel immediately emerge as the two emblematic locations for lost opportunities. Bush's unconditional support of Israeli Prime Minister Ariel Sharon will have lasting effects, but it is unsure whether American electors will consider it that much in November. This is not the case for the Iraqi adventure, especially after the official 1000 headcount of US soldiers killed in Iraq was reached last week (not to mention the 7000 wounded). "Mission accomplished" in Iraq: 1000 dead, US$200 billion spent and "no money for a social security programme", Kerry has just said. This may be how the Iraqi debate comes back to the US. Whether Bush lied or not over the existence of weapons of mass destruction will only have a mitigating effect, as the American elector seems to believe that the President "honestly" thought that the threat was real. On the contrary, the non-existent link between 9/11, terrorism and Saddam Hussein will be more difficult for electors to swallow, for it is a lasting lie. Indeed, US soldiers fighting in Iraq have not yet been told that they are not there, as they still believe, to carry out an act of revenge and defeat the terrorists. Nor is dying for more oil a good argument to provide soldiers with. But as a result of the war, Iraq has now concentrated the hard core of terrorism within its borders. Cities supposedly freed by the US troops have fallen under the control of ultra-Islamists, Baathists and others. Instability is set to continue on for another ten years, whereas any new development seems to turn sour. As an example, the June "handover of sovereignty" was supposed to be a new start for the Americans and a way for the Iraqis to take their future in hand. But Iraqis in command are not part of Iraqi society. During the Najaf events, an eight-member delegation headed by Sheikh Hussein Al Sad, went to convince Moqtada Al Sadr to leave the city, depose arms and create a political party to join the "democratic process". They arrived on a US military base, using helicopters and armoured vehicles of the US army in the name of the Iraqi government. Who would have listened to them? Finally, Moqtada

Al Sadr left the place with his people and their arms. With no winners or losers, the emergence of an Iraqi solution brokered by Shiite Grand Ayatollah Ali Sistani was another blow to local American policy.

The US has created a disaster in Iraq and they do not know how to deal with it. And when they decided to attack the city of Latiffya the very day French hostages were due to be freed, it was never likely that co-operation between Western allies would be reinforced. Iraqi Prime Minister and CIA-enrolled Iyad Allawi launched a fierce attack against French President Jacques Chirac last week. He made fun of these French "having an illusion if they hoped they could stay out of terrorism", as if France had not already paid a heavy tribute to terrorism. Nevertheless, a few days ago he turned back to France and asked for its support against "terrorists" (actually, everybody but Allawi and colleagues). The point here is that the apparent Iraqi (although US-sponsored) Administration that arrived in Baghdad in American suitcases will never convince the Iraqi people that they talk on their behalf. The current dilemma for Iraqi officials is whether to gain legitimacy with their people (which means they will have to oppose the Americans) or to forget about it (which means they will be of no use to the Americans). When looking at the daily growing unrest in Iraq and the climbing toll of civilian casualties, it is more than time for the Americans to reverse their policy and reconsider their presence there; and for the Iraqis, to initiate a true political process before it is too late.

POSING WRONG QUESTIONS ABOUT A TRUE CRISIS

27 September 2004

Forty days ago, two French journalists and their Syrian driver were kidnapped in Iraq on their way from Baghdad to Najaf. A series of communiqués leads us to believe that they are in the hands of one of the fundamentalist groups that is now fighting the American occupation in Iraq. An all-out diplomacy involving the leaders of the French Muslim community and the many Arab friends that France has in the region did its best to resolve the crisis. Yet, a month and a half later, the situation remains very much as it was at the beginning. A flurry of communication, a few mistakes and undoubtedly a pretty unfortunate military action by the US army the very day a positive outcome was expected did not help. Today, two facts are certain. The first is that many aspects of this sad story remain unknown. Why were these people abducted? What kind of manipulation was exercised (all kinds of rumours are now circulating in chancelleries)? How did the "Muslim veil" issue come into an Iraqi picture that probably had other more compelling issues to deal with? And finally, who profits from this crime? These questions remain unanswered and honest analysts acknowledge that they still miss too many clues. The other element is that, under such circumstances, the better the discretion, the larger the chances of success.

Unfortunately, this is not the way some "friends" of France look at the matter. In short, an argument raised by American neo-conservatives, notably in the columns of the *Wall Street Journal*, is that the French so-called "Arab policy" was designed to keep French interest safe from any kind of terrorism by "Islamists". This was also brought forward by their man on the spot, US-appointed Prime Minister Iyad Allawi. A deeper justification of that policy would be the existence of an important Muslim community in France and, therefore, the need for France to maintain good relations with the Islamic world.

Hence the supposed complete lack of interest from the French government towards the other non-French hostages, or the remark by

Allawi according to which the French would have succumbed to the fatal illusion of believing that they would escape terrorism if they adopted a specific pro-Arab policy. In this regard, he should be reminded that, for a long time, France has been a victim of terrorism, as terrorist attacks in Paris's St Michel subway[1] and others can testify. The rest is insignificant, because everybody knows where it comes from.

On the other hand, the reasons for a French pro-Arab policy are worth highlighting. Among others, General Charles de Gaulle prepared this U-turn in French foreign policy in the 1960s in consideration of the traditional presence of French interest in the Arab world, the specific nature of the relationship with the countries of North Africa and the invasion of Palestine by Israel in 1967. But it's more interesting to examine the matter today under the spectrum of a large presence of Muslim citizens in France. As IFRI analyst Dominique Moïsi recently wrote in an article in Britain's *Financial Times*: "The question remains whether France is committing a terrible mistake by pursuing, for essentially domestic reasons, its dialogue with Islam." And his answer is that a fair position is to stand between an American hard line neo-conservative's vision, which rightfully emphasises the universal threat of the Islamic fundamentalism, and a French pursuit of dialogue and *rapprochement*. Hence "an agonising test" that France would now face.

This presentation of the situation is not only intellectually contestable, it is simply appalling. To start with, how can one peacefully write that a "terrible mistake" may derive from "pursuing [a] dialogue with Islam"? Does the simple fact of pursuing a dialogue give room for it to be contested, or is it talking "with Islam" that is contested? None of them, we hope. But the underlying fact is even more dramatic as, once again, words prove to be the new weapons of mass destruction of the 21st century. In a mere five-line phrase, Moïsi starts talking of "Islam", then adds that "Islamism is the threat" and concludes with "dealing with terrorism and Islamic fundamentalism". All the ingredients of an intellectual manipulation are gathered together: "Islam", "Islamic fundamentalism" and "terrorism". Each concept follows the other one in a mechanical chain that straightforwardly concludes with a more simple motto: Fight the Muslims.

Like any human situation, that of French citizens of Muslim religion shows a far greater contrast than these observers seem to think. Is it necessary to claim that not all Islamic fundamentalists are terrorists, that not all Muslims are fundamentalists or, should we dare suggest, that many terrorists are not Muslim? But it is so simple to call for making a "common cause against barbarism", as the neo-conservative review *Weekly Standard*'s editor William Kristol wrote in a recent issue. It seems so profitable to Israeli Vice Prime Minister Ehud Olmert to make the innocents murdered from Bali to Istanbul, from Jerusalem to Madrid, from Fallujah and beyond seem to be "Yasser Arafat's legacy". Doing so has been Israeli behaviour for years, according to which "he who is not with me is a terrorist". Why should we feel compelled to tolerate this culture of death?

The French hostage crisis is a terrible sequence in our country's daily life. Let the competent people work with the discretion that is required. But we must be attentive not to let all kinds of fanatics mix up everything, establish new separation lines according to what they think is good or bad, and finally pursue unnoticed their dark projects.

Notes

1   On 25 July 1995 Islamist terrorists belonging to the Islamic Algerian Group (GIA) exploded a bomb in the subway station of Saint Michel in central Paris, killing eight and wounding many others. Other attacks took place afterwards, notably in October (Orsay and Maison Blanche subway station, wounding about 50 people). GIA was extending the scope of a fight it has started against the military government in Algeria at that time to France. Since then, GIA has transformed into another terrorist organisation that is said to have links with Al Qaida.

FIGHTING AN ENEMY WITHOUT IDENTIFYING IT FIRST

11 OCTOBER 2004

Terrorism is the new plague of the 21st century. It has become a global threat that everyone should fight resolutely. To be efficient, "the war against terrorism" cannot be limited to a simple aphorism common to every situation. The concept itself is complex and its recent proponents require lengthy expositions.

As history shows, the word "terrorism" is relatively new to us. It expressed an extreme and indiscriminate violence perpetrated by individuals (states preferably being accused of "war crimes"). The French Revolution (1792–95) was a so-called "Terror" and its leader, Maximilien Robespierre, a "terrorist". Apart from a few isolated cases in the 1800s, it was the wars of independence that witnessed the use of the word. Combatants became "terrorists" until they become "national heroes" once independence had been gained. While the French Resistance in the Second World War were considered "terrorists" to the Nazis, nobody claimed that America was a "terrorist state" when it indiscriminately carpet bombed civilians and soldiers in Vietnam. Libya or Israel may, for different reasons, have assented to the status of political actors practising a "state terrorism", but the word was more commonly used for all those laying down bombs – from Corsican activists to IRA soldiers and from Basque separatists to the Red Army Brigades. However, due to its diversified content, no one would have thought of using the same means in order to resolve the Northern Ireland conflict or the fight against the Bader Meinhoff gang in Germany.

The existence of terrorism in a democracy is an insult to the freely expressed choice of a majority, whereas fighting for independence calls for other considerations. There is a difference between imposing one's view by force and fighting for freedom. While some methods of action can be identical ("terrorists" use the means they have which are not usually those of a nation), tactical alliances can also be woven. Yet a difference can be made according to the situation, and fights for independence are usually viewed differently.

So how has terrorism progressively become a global phenomenon? In the aftermath of the Palestinian uprising, any fighter using extreme violence has been put on the list of "terrorist". For now, anyone who opposes a dominant power will soon be put on that list. Whoever fights Israeli expansionism is labelled a potential terrorist. Look at the 12 UN officials arrested last week in Occupied Jerusalem. Listen to Russia's president Vladimir Putin talking of Chechnya nationalist fighters (forgetting the thousands of civilians deported in cattle trucks by Josef Stalin during the winter of 1944). And were not the matter so serious, reflect on Richard Perle's accusation of "terrorism" against those journalists who dared to investigate one of the many embezzlements he has been part of. Except for the remarkable achievement of Bush, who was able to unite all the anti-coalition components in Iraq, it is clearly of interest to the established powers to favour an alliance that enables co-operation between nations to fight a common enemy.

That the actions of the Zionists are quickly approved by American neo-conservatives is a sad example of what manipulation can achieve. It allows Israel, in a recent example, to kill dozens of innocent people while the rest of the world stays quiet, as it has been doing for the past two weeks during its Gaza Strip incursions. Two hundred children were murdered in the Belsan school, Russia; thousands of civilians were gassed with napalm during the Vietnam conflict and in Iraq; nearly 3000 people were killed in the 9/11 World Trade Center and Pentagon attacks, and 4400 Palestinians have been shot dead since Ariel Sharon's stroll into the compound of Al Haram Al Quds Al Sharif. All this may lead one to believe it is only the number of victims that differs and reaction can only be a total condemnation of such acts. But what will the result of fighting global terrorism be to the birth of new terrorists replacing those who died or were jailed, as if evil could be extruded from the person and the disease cured through the killing of the patient?

At the end of the day, terrorism must be fought. As Pope John Paul II said: "Violence breeds violence; it is a no-exit road." But he added shortly after that "one should address the roots", since no one solution ever answered every situation.

Some actions can be taken in unison, such as the gathering and sharing of sensitive information, but no action will ever succeed if the underlying reason for the terrorist act is not addressed. First, there must be an analysis of the cause. The conflicts in Northern Ireland, Palestine or Chechnya still need to be solved by means other than fighting. Any indiscriminate action will only result in the emergence of a unified terrorist front, threats of dimensions other than Al Qaida, as Iraq shows. Ignoring an appraisal of the underlying elements to terrorist action will ultimately lead only to more terrorism. As long as Russian soldiers deny Chechens the right to independence, or Israeli soldiers continue to humiliate Palestinians striking whom and when they want in the Occupied Territories, there will be terrorism. The alternative is to kill all Chechens and Palestinians. Is this what the "civilised world" wants? Some policies are doing as much to create new terrorists as they are to end terrorism. In the wait for governments to reflect and not succumb to the manipulations of those who abide by partisan considerations, let me conclude with a remark by Professor Lawrence Freedman of London's Centre for Security Analysis, Kings College: "In the end, the best way to deal with evil leaders is to provide people with few reasons to follow them."

EUROPE AND THE US SHOULD FORM A SYMBIOTIC RELATIONSHIP

25 OCTOBER 2004

There are still a few days to go before the result of the latest US "beauty contest" is known. Biased opinion polls and arrogance on both sides have not helped anyone decide who will win. But in the end, does it really matter?

Whoever wins will have to address the same issues as the previous incumbent, and with apparently similar means at his disposal. There is the economic situation, with huge trade and budget deficits, rising inflation, poor creation of jobs, net balance decreasing for the first time since 1930, overall fragile growth and no social cover for 45 million Americans. There is the need to define an efficient policy to fight terrorism and establish an exit strategy in Iraq, which does not seem to offer much room for manoeuvre. But right now, all we can do is wonder what will happen next Tuesday on the other side of the Atlantic.

At first it may seem that there is no difference between John F. Kerry and George W. Bush, and it will not matter who wins. The belief is that issues will be dealt with the same way in either case. Yet, somewhat naively, many Europeans (not to say the whole world) would still vote for Kerry. The Europeans, 73 per cent of whom believe they live in a more dangerous world since the Iraq invasion, think that with Kerry in command the US unilateralist attitude will change. But Bush's supporters claim that Kerry has no miracle solution in hand. ("The US foreign policy cannot change overnight. It is in Iraq a fait accompli. If Kerry is elected, he won't have the means to shift it," declared Defence Policy Board member Richard Allen in Paris last week.)

The candidates express similar views on a number of issues. (Guess who said: "The fence has proven its value as an anti-terror measure ... We will never compromise America's special relationship with our ally Israel and I will never pressure Israel to make concessions that will compromise its security." It was Kerry.) But in general a change of president is not enough to create any new differences to those that have emerged over recent years between the US and Europe. There is the usual conflict of interest in commerce (agriculture, and aeronautics as the latest rift over Boeing and Airbus has shown). Yet two major events may now change the situation. The first is the disappearance of the communist threat, which worked as a bond between the western allies. The second is the 9/11 attacks, which made the US re-focus its international strategy on national security. Whatever Kerry intends to do abroad, especially in Iraq or Palestine, he will never have a free hand if Americans think he is putting their security at risk. The search for absolute sovereignty and full security, as well as the prevalence of unilateralism, are now deep-rooted within the American psyche.

Reviewing the issues that are pulling America and Europe apart with the hope that Kerry would lean towards Europe has now become irrelevant. While a Kerry election may help change the tune and make people return to the table, yet, some of Bush's supporters say that the president will change both team and behaviour. Should Europe remain passive and wait for the outcome of a discussion between neo-conservatives and neo-realists that it cannot join anyway? The answer is no. On the basis of shared interests, Europe needs to rationalise its relationship with the US, without being nostalgic or aggressive. It has to move forward and offer America a revised framework of practical measures for discussion.

President Jacques Chirac and Chancellor Gerhard Schroeder must team up with Britain's Prime Minister Tony Blair. This is also of interest to Blair. "The traffic on Mr Blair's fabled bridge across the Atlantic is too often one-way ... Britain must rebuild its relationship with the big powers of Europe ... because it needs friends on both sides of the Atlantic," writes Philip Stephens in Britain's *Financial Times*. Then, as former French foreign minister Hubert Védrinne argued recently:

> Europe should not be taken by surprise. It should make its own proposals immediately upon his election, to the new American president: world security, re-launching of the peace process in the Middle East, the future of Iraq, the fight against terrorism, re-legitimisation of the UN ...

Discussions may be difficult. When *Washington Post*'s Charles Krauthammer says that "re-engaging in a peace process [in the Middle East] is like giving into Europeans on Israel", it's pretty obvious that is not going to be an easy road. But it is the only one that could re-establish a dialogue between the world's two most powerful blocs and incidentally revive a political Europe weakened by the successful American divide on Iraq. The alternative is more confusion among allies, friends and "former friends", more arrogance and, ultimately, more violence.

Whoever the winner is (and some outcomes may be easier to handle than others), this American election finally represents a great opportunity for Europe to show the rest of the world that it can come up with manageable solutions and hold its rank. But time is running short.

FRANCE HAS LOST A VERY CLOSE FRIEND

3 NOVEMBER 2004

George W. Bush, it seems, has just been re-elected President of the United States. The same day, the United Arab Emirate's much-admired ruler, Shaikh Zayed Bin Sultan Al Nahyan, passed away. History sometimes stammers.

By passing away, ordinary statesmen remind their people of their achievements, their worth, and sometimes their failures. When it comes to exceptional statesmen, the list often reads like a graduation ceremony. But when it comes to beloved and cherished statesmen, then the throat gets dry and sobbing is hard to control, emotions not easy to restrain. The people of the UAE have lost a father, the Arab world a wise man and France a friend.

The list of exceptional achievements of Shaikh Zayed is a long one. It spreads over 33 years, a period during which, as the ruler of Abu Dhabi in 1966 and President of the UAE since 1971, a relatively poorly educated country has seen spectacular development and fantastic growth. Pushing limits, it has become what it is today – a success story and undisputed leader in many fields. There is no other explanation for the love and devotion people have shown towards Shaikh Zayed, which is a rather unique phenomenon in the region. Not only was Shaikh Zayed loved by his people because he gave them what anyone would look for, but also because he had many qualities that make the difference between great leaders and "the rest". He had been able to win the hearts and minds of people. He would counter arrogance, excitement and confusion with wisdom, moderation and balance. His role during the crisis that hit the region from time to time was based on the simple, although constant, guideline: let good sense prevail, find the contact point between the parties and help them to work out a balanced solution. A conciliatory tone, a statesmanlike demeanour, a charismatic presence ... indeed, some people are luckier than others.

The story of Shaikh Zayed is also the story of France in the region. The UAE–French relationship, which has strengthened over the years, did not get where it is today by chance. It was part of a wider political strategy that was underlined by the Co-operation and Defence Agreement signed between the UAE and France in 1995, and further enhanced in 1997 after the visit of French President Jacques Chirac to Abu Dhabi. This state visit, the highest level of contact in diplomatic terms, can indeed be seen as a new departure towards a strategic alliance, a partnership based on mutual trust. Similar views on many international issues brought Shaikh Zayed and Chirac closer. It is true to say that the relationship between two countries is often characterised by the volume of business exchange, numbers of contracts or the amount of capital flows, just as it would be between two private trade partners. In this respect, we can cite the expertise and competence of French companies, especially in the oil and gas fields, with names such as Total or Technip. But the relationship between France and the UAE, between Shaikh Zayed and Chirac, exceeded this necessary although trivial basis.

France never doubted the importance of Shaikh Zayed's opinion. It may not be commonly known, but Chirac is a man who listens to others, especially those whose wisdom and analytical abilities he appreciates. Chirac, in this respect, has had many occasions to show the consideration he held for the opinion of Shaikh Zayed. Chirac toured the region in November 2001, two months after 9/11. Of course, it was important at that time to know precisely what regional leaders had in mind, what they were anticipating and how they would react to the new situation in order to be able to deal with it accordingly. He thus decided to stop over in Cairo, in Riyadh ... and in the UAE – for there was no doubt in his mind that Shaikh Zayed was the person he had to listen to.

This, I believe, is worth much more than any long speech about the traditional friendship between our two peoples, the volume of trade between our companies or the potential for new enterprises to be led jointly in the future in fields such as tourism and banking. Today, France wants to remember; France is mourning the death of a friend. We all know there is little to say in such circumstances, but we must stay silent and suffer together. These are the most sincere condolences we can offer our UAE friends.

DOLLAR IS SINKING AS DEFICIT MOUNTS

8 NOVEMBER 2004

The US dollar hit a record level of 1.3007 against the euro last Wednesday and is now hovering at around 1.2970. It is amazing that the greenback slumped to this all-time low so soon after Washington released its monthly statistics on jobs creation. The report suggested that the country had created 337,000 jobs in October, which it felt was "good". If that was the case, then why did the markets react so badly? Probably it is sending a message – that is, American consumers will spend more and save less, thereby pushing the trade deficit further into the red. It now represents 5.5 per cent of the gross domestic product (GDP), a figure of US$415 billion over the past 12 months.

With the exception of the *Wall Street Journal*'s George Melloan, who feels that "the American economy runs well", an increasing number of economists around the world, including the US, are issuing more and more warnings. The facts are clear. The US current account deficit – that is, the excess of what Americans spend on goods, services and funds transferred abroad over which the US earns from the rest of the world – now exceeds US$500 billion, which amounts to 5 per cent of the GDP. That is the result of the above-mentioned trade deficit, in spite of the currency having already lost nearly 30 per cent of its value against the euro over one year. This is an excessive consumption (the saving ratio in the US is 2 per cent compared to an average 10–15 per cent in the rest of the developed world) and a bad fiscal policy (the budget deficit alone represents 3 per cent of the GDP). The results are also as clear. Just to take the position of the Asian Central Banks, their US financial assets now exceed US$124 billion. The US has to find US$2 billion per day just to close the balance. How long will that last?

As usual for economic issues, the theories are conflicting. "America's current account deficit is not only sustainable, it is perfectly logical given the world's hunger for investment returns and dollar reserves," writes Richard Cooper, former US Undersecretary of State for Economic

Affairs, in Britain's *Financial Times*. His main argument is that this situation can go on for years (he cites a 15-year period) as long as the growth continues. Considering that the US economy accounts for more than one-quarter of the global economy and provides a higher return on investment than any other developed country, other savers will continue to invest in the US whatever the front value of the dollar. On the opposite side, two university professors from Berkeley and Harvard answer Cooper and ask: "Should the US Administration worry that the US is single-handedly eating up more than 70 per cent of the combined current account surpluses of China, Japan, Germany and all other surplus countries in the world? Our answer is a resounding 'Yes'." In theoretical fields, it happens often that when a situation moves towards a predicted catastrophe which has not yet occurred, new theories explain that since it did not occur, the underlying conditions for it may go on for years with nothing to fear. This is, of course, until the catastrophe actually happens.

A fair analysis of the American economy can only lead to some basic evidence. Americans do not pay enough taxes to cover the cost of their public spending. They import much more than what they sell abroad. They do not save enough and consume too much. As a result, the rest of the world finances US consumers so that they can go on consuming, importing and creating new jobs related to their own spending. But are these "good" jobs? Is this a "real" growth based on factual wealth-creating economic realities? Is it true to say that this is made possible because the US itself prints the currency that it borrows, or that the US pays in dollars the energy it needs to import? But in concrete Treasury terms, the US must place US$2 billion every day with foreign financial institutions, the reserves of which are not without limits. For the time being, it works the same as it does for those investors who enjoy the benefits of an over-performing market and only decide to leave it or diversify their holdings once it is too late. Actually, it looks like something such as a perfusion: the day it stops inadvertently, the sick man doesn't steadily get worse; he collapses immediately. It is why no soft-landing should be expected from a decreasing dollar (just imagine that bringing down the trade deficit to 3.5 per cent of GDP would already cost the dollar another 35 per cent in value). The currency will actually fall abruptly and sharply. US authorities will then have no other choice but to raise interest rates, quickly and significantly, creating as a result recession in America and all over the world. This is what will happen unless corrective measures are taken, immediately.

"A sober US president-elect ought to worry a lot about his country's foreign borrowing addiction," the two professors wrote. But it is not sure that George W. Bush will care. As well as "promoting freedom and democracy in the world" the way we know, his new programme also provides for new fiscal policies that, on the contrary, will increase the public deficit. A war in Iraq costing US$1 billion per week – a new request for US$70 billion has now reached the US Congress – will not help either. In the ferocious environment of US capitalism and its shady financial markets (MCI, Enron and others), this is not what is needed by America. Nor by the rest of the world.

NOTHING HAS CHANGED WITH ARAFAT'S DEATH

22 November 2004

Two things are taken for granted in Europe about the Israeli–Palestinian conflict: the necessary removal of Yasser Arafat for peace to progress; and the positive impact of the unilateral withdrawal from the Gaza Strip by Israeli Prime Minister Ariel Sharon. Both ideas, however, are dramatically wrong.

"The passing from the political scene of the Palestinian leader may be what is needed to bring the peace process in the Middle East back to life," writes Britain's weekly *The Economist*. With Arafat out of the way, the Americans and Israelis will have no more choice nor an excuse to return to the negotiating table. After the Palestinian leader passed away, the recurrent US epitaph was: "Arafat was no partner for peace". In a greatly co-operative mood, the United States then told the Palestinians to choose their next leader from among Mahmoud Abbas and Ahmed Qorei. Sharon, whose country did everything it could to assassinate credible Palestinian leaders, was more cautious. "It is needless to rush into the arms of new Palestinian leaders," he said, "before they give evidence of their good faith." As usual, Israel will discuss its own requirements, irrespective of what its population may think or say. Too bad for President George W. Bush, who is desperately seeking an elected leader to pursue his Middle East initiative. "The entire responsibility of peace bears on the Palestinian's desire to build a democracy," Bush said. If that is the case, then let's start with a free process, a mechanism whereby Israelis do not choose the candidates, nor dictate the voters' list. Let us raise the voting rights issue of those electors located in the Eastern sector of Occupied Jerusalem, or acknowledge the unavoidable position of some actors such as Hamas. And then, when the Palestinian people decide, one will see whether Sharon wishes peace or not.

On the occasion of the Israeli parliament approving Sharon's disengagement plan from the Gaza Strip last October, a few people with good faith praised the decision. No matter what his true motives were, they asked the world to "swallow its natural scepticism" and help Sharon's view prevail. Indeed, his past actions could insinuate that the withdrawal was only a ruse but, in fact, the evacuation process would have larger benefits for the population such as improving their living conditions, relying on Israel to open Gaza's airport and seaport, and offering the Palestinians the ability to establish law and order. For the first time since 1967, Israel was giving up territories it occupied by force and such occasions could not be missed.

But this dream vision is being confronted by a harsh and different reality for at least three reasons. First, this unilateral disengagement is imposed in their own home on a population that is treated as a passive witness, with no right to intervene. No mention of the occupied West Bank was ever made. It is thus not difficult to predict that this evacuation will turn Gaza into a prison since, at the same time, Israel reinforces protection of its massive colonies in the West Bank and continues to build the separation wall. Second, the conditions of the evacuation (whereby there is no preliminary discussion with the Palestinian authority in order to organise the transfer of powers) leave an open road to violence: Hamas's unlikely disarmament, the continuation of violence in the other Occupied Territories and impossible administration of what Americans call a "Palestinian laboratory" – "The Palestinian people must govern themselves and prove to the world that they are ready for statehood," says former US envoy Dennis Ross. Such writing will obviously make the experience fail. That, actually, will last as long as the Israelis will create the conditions for the Palestinian chaos. The Israelis ask the Palestinians to continue with reforms, but when they try they are prevented from doing so by the same Israelis. The third reason is Sharon's track record. He has an uninterrupted list of actions aimed at sabotaging any idea of an independent and viable Palestinian state. A final touch was given by Sharon's lawyer and advisor Dov Weisglass in a recent interview with Israel's daily *Haaretz* whereby the beauty of disengaging from Gaza would be to remove Palestinian statehood indefinitely from Israel's agenda while doing the minimum possible.

Actually, nothing will change in Occupied Palestine for as long as there's no complete change of method. How can Palestine Foreign Affairs Minister Nabil Chaath transform the Gaza withdrawal into "the first step of the roadmap" after Weisglass's comments or Bush's hopes "to see a Palestinian state, but not before 2009"? Over the past 50 years,

Israelis and Palestinians have been fighting too much to believe that they could now just sit down and talk together. The vision of people learning to know each other and maybe live side by side has failed, and the roadmap process is just another avatar of that vision. The step-by-step approach is dead because any global agreement will always be the result of a compromise made of mutual concessions. It will thus have to be implemented globally, and with immediate effect for good and by force, that is by an international force obviously headed by the US and supported in the first place by other interested parties. These should include Arab countries in the region, Europe and Russia. Everybody knows that with the settlement of the Israeli–Palestinian conflict, the terrorists won't have any reason to hate the West. It is thus in the best interests of the West to take the necessary action. At the same time, the United States should understand that it is unlikely that the world's sole super-power can solve the Middle East conflict on its own.

THERE IS NO EXIT STRATEGY FOR THE UNITED STATES IN IRAQ

6 December 2004

The American media believes there will be a fairy-tale ending to the Iraqi occupation once the elections are held and a new constitution comes into force. The general elections to be organised in Iraq next January will elect 275 new members to parliament. The transitory assembly will then draft a new constitution by 15 August and will control the government until new elections take place on 10 October. In the meantime, the US troops will have begun to withdraw and a democratic Iraq will be born. That is what the American press is saying. But the truth is different. The elections, if they take place, will be all but democratic. Whatever the result, which is already known, it will change nothing in what is left of occupied Iraq. America is in a trap and will remain in it as long as it wants to make it alone.

The conference of Sharm al Shaikh held on 22 and 23 November was the final chance to make credible preparations for the vote, and for all the delegates to set aside their past differences and unite for the election plan. However, not all the interested parties were invited. In the case of representatives from Fallujah, the American army was removing the possibility of having the Sunnis join the process. Actually, the Sharm al Shaikh meeting achieved nothing and the election boycott will go ahead. The major point is not the boycott of the elections announced by 47 Iraqi political parties, but that for the US, Iraqi anti-democratic forces, Sunnis and terrorists are one and the same. Where is democracy when each of the leading ethnic groups tries to dominate the other and grab power? Be they Shiite, Kurds or Sunnis, each of them is trying to out-manoeuvre the other. So what does it matter whether the majority of Iraqis are Shiites? This is no problem for the United States simply because they only care about the Shiites being officially invested with a popular vote. "It's true that the majority Shiites are likely to dominate the new parliament, but that was anticipated from the minute the international coalition decided to topple Saddam Hussein and his Sunni clique," reports the *Wall Street Journal.* Other Sunni populations in the region will acquiesce.

In the meantime, violence continues unabated. America no longer has control over the situation, as the latest attack in the heart of the Baghdad's Green zone proves. As in Fallujah, "the fact that Americans are having to fight so fiercely inside a major city, 18 months after liberating Iraq from Saddam Hussein, is a sign of how close Mr Bush's Iraq policy is teetering towards failure", writes Britain's weekly *The Economist.* Terror, unrest and kidnappings are the daily lot suffered by a population who thought that democracy and security go hand in hand. However, America has failed in that mission. It is said that 15,000 additional US troops are heading for Iraq, but this will never be sufficient to control the violence in Iraq. A military solution to the American presence in Iraq would mean increasing the present 135,000 forces to 550,000 or 600,000 troops.

The US exit strategy from Iraq is actually deadlocked. The military option means that the United States would be ready to impose by force their presence on a foreign country which doesn't welcome it. According to the United States' front-man in Iraq, Iyad Allawi, among the 20,000 or so insurgents, the number of foreigners would not exceed 1000. The occupation has now become a war of national liberation. There is little doubt that half a million foreign soldiers in Iraq can maintain a certain order, but besides the cost the insurgency is not something that will end in a couple of months. Indeed, leaving the place right now will instantly create further chaos. There is neither a working administration nor representative government, and the population will be left dramatically unattended. An article in *The Economist* says: "Unelected Allawi, lacking enough loyal soldiers of his own, is in the end a creature of the Americans." A man put in place by an occupying army with no legitimacy has never been reasonably considered a valuable interlocutor. But the new element is that the United States starts saying it. "Allawi didn't start with much of a domestic constituency," reports the *Wall Street Journal,* which is an interesting signal of the support the United States extends to its sycophants when it does not need them any more.

It is likely that a solution could have been worked out a year ago through initiating a truly political process within the legal framework of the international community. Under a clear mandate by the UN, a real coalition could have stepped in, restored security and, most likely, split administrative issues – to be looked at immediately – from political matters which could have been addressed in a second step. "History shows that elections do not create democracies," writes Ralph Dahrendorf of the London School of Economics, "as they are not the first but the last steps of democracy." Weighted elections under international supervision could also have been arranged once a new administration process was put in place. But this is too late because the United States took the terrible responsibility of playing it differently, and there is no need either to lament further. For once, the US Secretary of State designate Condoleezza Rice should now try to analyse the Iraqi situation. Her constant intellectual references over the years – with regards the Cold War and the situation in Germany in 1945 – can work to her advantage. In that respect, she can call for the internationalisation of Iraq with direct administration under the auspices of the international community and return to law and order before a political process takes place.

But "American power has never been able to understand the positive effects of dependence on others," writes Philip Stephens in Britain's *Financial Times*. The cost of it in Iraq will be further chaos, terrorism and, ultimately, partition. Living in a safer world, are we ready for that?

FRENCH RIFT WITH THE US COULD SPREAD ACROSS EUROPE

20 December 2004

Ignore Germany, forgive Russia and punish France. This remark made by United States Secretary of State designate Condoleezza Rice after the US invaded Iraq ought to characterize the new relationship between America and France. Thomas Friedman, in *The New York Times*, went a step further: "France is not only an irritating ally or a jealous rival. It has become an enemy of the US." The good old days of Benjamin Franklin – a second ambassador in Paris – are gone. He once wrote: "Nothing should be spared to keep France [as] our ally; France is the only country on which one can rely under every event. The French seem to love us more than they do any other nation on earth." What happened to the world's only super-power and a medium-sized European country that shared so much in the past? Two months before US President George W. Bush comes to Europe and thinks of repairing the damaged relationship between the US and Europe – notably with Germany and France – two viewpoints come to mind. First, the damage might be deeper than people like British Prime Minister Tony Blair may think; indeed, it would seem he prefers that differences be put aside as if nothing has happened. Second, and more likely, the rift may spread to the whole of Europe in its long but unabated march towards becoming a world power.

The French, it is said, would be genetically affected by a deeply anti-American feeling, an underlying characteristic of French political life. The point, actually, is that the French do not like Bush's policies. This goes far beyond the usual clichés about conflicting missionary visions, or recurrent fights in the fields of aeronautics, defence equipment, energy, foodstuff or agriculture. Even if the French drop their supposedly anti-American rhetoric, there would still be no reason why France should have not "the legitimate historical and cultural reasons to assert itself in the world, the right to press home its commercial advantage or perceive its interest as being different from America's", as noted by *The Economist*. Something else has dragged the relationship to where it is now.

Comments by the *Wall Street Journal* and other neo-conservative media shed some light, with formulas such as the "European Union's billions of euros of illegal subsidies propping up ailing French national champions", "France is the hole in the European donut of power policies today" or "France today lags Italy in demonstrating military combat resolve" (Jim Hoagland). But these are just insults. On the contrary, what is changing the framework is a growing and systematic use of false evidence. In the Middle East, 18 months after the US military invasion of Iraq, the democratic reshuffling promised by Bush – a justification for going to war – has not taken place. It hasn't even started. No Arab regime was overthrown, in spite of the situation each of them must now face because of US policies As for Iran, manipulation goes on and follows the same Iraqi pre-war pattern: about the nuclear threat, with the use of unproven allegations aimed at instilling doubts.

By-passing a local situation's complexity in its search for "one single viable model of national success, worthwhile for each individual in any society" (Rice), the Bush Administration subordinates all its decisions to the "global war on terror"; a concept whose definition is unclear, with its limits fluctuating according to circumstance. In Guantanamo the torture of detainees goes on, something noted not only by the International Committee of the Red Cross but also by America's own FBI. Abu Ghraib's drama was hardly sanctioned; Bush's former legal advisor, Alberto Gonzales, the person who wrote the famous memo about "how far" it is possible to question a prisoner, has just been promoted to Justice Secretary. Why would it be different when columnists like George Melloan, making some observations about choosing a leader, come back on "peripheral issues too unimportant to merit presidential attention. Abu Ghraib was blown up as a big scandal, when what really happened was that some Iraqi prisoners, themselves guilty of who knows what atrocities, were 'humiliated' "? Let's add the imaginary balanced approach to the Israeli–Palestinian conflict, the equivocal role played by the US with Arab states in the region, and one will understand why the relationship with America has become so difficult – especially when the matter has now widened to the whole of Europe.

A recurrent element of America's divide-and-rule policy in Europe is to underline France's "weakening hand" or the fact that "the Franco-German era of driving the EU agenda is over". It is obvious that the Europe France helped create is changing fast, and according to simple arithmetic, Paris is losing its dominant grip. But France is also vital to Europe, as is the Franco–German axis which, incidentally, resisted American pressure. The rest of Europe, notably Spain and Poland, is now following suit. Europe is also changing its philosophy. The Federalist option of some members has been diluted and a gathering of powerful nations could, in the future, use Europe more and more as a lever. This is the true meaning of the "Power Europe" vision that is not an endless strengthening process by politically irresponsible civil servants in Brussels, but a sharing of means by strong nations aimed at yielding an even greater advantage for the whole group. This inescapable process will turn Europe into one of the world's power centres, a role "that [she has] not yet fully played but which should be hers", according to former US National Security Advisor Zbigniew Brzezinski. "The more Europe will be able to bring proofs of its unity and military strength on the negotiations table, the more Washington will better adjust its policy in order to make sure of the European help. Bush can go on hiding in his ideological bunker, [but] the need to share the job with other forces in the world is becoming more and more obvious," writes Georgetown University Professor Charles Kopchan. This evidence seems to have missed Bush's wife Laura who, during the election campaign, praised the "willing" America acting "in a decisive way to win over terrorism and spread freedom". When we move past the old rhetoric of empty words and disastrous results, repairing the old relationship between the US and Europe may start again. But it may need another four years.

2005

WORKING FOR A FUTURE

Timeline World News 2005

January:	Mahmoud Abbas wins Palestinian presidential election.
30 January:	8 million people vote in election in Iraq. Majority is won by the Shia United Iraqi, with Kurdish parties coming second in polls.
February:	Sharm Al Shaikh meeting.
13 February:	Bush visits Europe.
14 February:	Murder of Rafiq Hariri in Lebanon.
28 February:	In the worst incident since the US-led invasion of Iraq, over 100 people are killed in Baghdad by a huge car bomb.
18 March:	Publication of the Sasson report.
April:	Iraqi parliament chooses Kurdish leader Jalal Talabani as new president. Shia Ibrahim Jaafari becomes prime minister.
May:	Iran begins talks with World Trade Organization to become a member.
5 May:	Tony Blair is re-elected as Prime Minister.
29 May:	French fail to ratify EU treaty.

KIND WISHES ALONE WILL NOT BE ENOUGH FOR THE NEW YEAR

3 JANUARY 2005

How is it that a routine, traditional exercise this year has become something that nobody feels willing to believe in any longer? Extending wishes for a happy 2005 after what happened in South-East Asia requires optimism. Thinking of what may happen next in the region requires faith, for tsunamis and earthquakes can also be of a political nature.

In Asia, the world learnt with stupor that a gigantic wave triggered by an earthquake that took place off the edge of Sumatra could be left unnoticed until it drowned hundreds of thousands of people. Actually, satellites were able to spot it, but the information was not relayed. This cannot happen any more in the Pacific ocean, because countries around it, such as the United States, Japan and Australia, have set up an observation centre of their own on the island of Hawaii. Good for them. But for the rest of humanity, for the less rich and famous, only the future is in their hands. It has now been made public that the United Nations will begin to implement a similar warning system for the Indian ocean – the UN, a useless instrument, as US President George W. Bush's neo-conservative press used to say. Regrets are a mere consolation once a tragic event has occurred. Still, everybody should feel ashamed after what happened. Exact figures may never be known; the death toll has already crossed the 150,000 mark but experts believe that with 5 million people migrating under the present circumstances, the casualty rate may rise by 10 per cent. On the other hand, one can easily imagine the suffering and destruction that could have been avoided to a certain extent had a monitoring system been installed. The cost of such a system would probably have been a thousandth of what, for instance, the American army spends each week in Iraq.

Globalisation, it seems, only works for the wealthiest. International co-operation is what is left to the poor. After a UN official described as "mean" the aid donations of the wealthiest countries in supplying international emergency aid, the United States reacted angrily. The director of USAid initiated a polemic with European countries and Secretary of State Colin Powell declared that "the US has given more aid these last four years than any other country in the world". Besides the fact that it is quite normal for the world's richest country to do so, one had better pay attention to the share of the gross national product that is spared for international aid. The US is last on the list of the 30 wealthiest countries, with a contribution of only 0.14 per cent of GNP against the 0.70 per cent targeted by the UN. How strikingly egoist the policy of this president must be for the *New York Times* to publish an editorial entitled "America, the Indifferent". But Bush was not inactive. His reaction to the tsunami drama was to create an international coalition of the willing. Let's hope it works better than previously.

News from the Middle East in the coming weeks is unlikely to make us optimistic. The elections in Iraq are a farce, and everybody knows it. The results will bring no political solution to a country that is falling day after day deeper into chaos. Dozens of casualties on the main roads of Iraqi cities now seem commonplace. One bit of good news emerged just before Christmas, to the despair of some lobbies. France's Middle East policy allowed it to rescue its hostages in Iraq. The support of Muslim organisations and Arab states in the region, coupled with active diplomacy, achieved an excellent result. But which positive next step can there be as long as the occupying forces behave the way they do?

In Occupied Palestine, British diplomacy was not as successful in its attempt to prevent Britain's Prime Minister Tony Blair from ridicule. "The mission had failed even before it started," Patrick Seale rightly noted in *Gulf News* (on 24 December). Now that the "international conference" has been downgraded to a "technical meeting" with Palestinians only, there is no more doubt about this. Let's face the reality: Israeli Prime Minister Ariel Sharon refuses to discuss any "final status" issues with anybody. Mahmoud Abbas's agenda is to obtain a truce from Hamas in order to strengthen his own power, to rebuild the Palestinian security forces and, perhaps, to initiate reforms before going back to the negotiating table. But Sharon wants to freeze the peace process, to withdraw from Gaza, to achieve the colonisation of the West Bank under the protection of the security wall and, ultimately, to render impossible the creation of a truly independent Palestinian state. This was explained at length by Sharon's advisor Dov Weisglass in his interview to the Israeli daily

Haaretz on 8 October 2004. Israel is not "a real partner for peace" and nothing successful was ever achieved in this conflict that was based on reciprocity.

If one puts aside Shimon Peres's intrusion – the Likud–Labor coalition will not survive one day after the Gaza Strip is evacuated – one can really wonder why Blair took the risk of being lampooned by a ridiculous Sharon. The Israeli Prime Minister has been selling the same stuff for years: "If a final end is put to terrorism, then my door will be opened to the roadmap." The day Israelis take full knowledge of the fact that there is no alternative for them other than the land-for-peace formula or the end of a fully Jewish state, the situation may change. It may nevertheless take a few more years of hatred and killings. No lonely initiatives or best wishes will be enough, for peace works as love: as the French poet Jean Cocteau said: "There is no love, but only proof of love."

ABU MAZEN'S BALANCING ACT IN PALESTINE

17 January 2005

The candidate favoured by United States President George W. Bush and Israeli Prime Minister Ariel Sharon has won the Palestinian presidential election. Mahmoud Abbas was not elected in spite of the American endorsement, but thanks to it. "Israel and the United States want Abu Mazen. Therefore, I will vote for him so that we can finally live in peace," said an old man after leaving a polling station. It is the kind of hope this election has created. The fall may be dramatic.

One can always argue about the freedom of elections held in Occupied Territories under the control of a foreign army. Arrested candidates, missing names on the lists, fear, checkpoints and barriers, there are more democratic ways to vote. However, stopping short of Bush's indecent appropriation of a "democratic" election – the Palestinians have their own track records on the matter and did not need Bush's meddling – nobody can honestly contest the reality of the choice expressed by the population. One prominent Palestinian businessman told me once: "The people are so tired; they are prepared to accept anything that will be given to them." Who could blame them?

Yet now that the twinkling dust of a debilitating unanimous way of thinking is fading away, what room for manoeuvre is left for Abbas? Nothing is very different than before his election. Western newspapers could not be more enthusiastic once the results were known; some even before they were. "A man of dialogue bearing the hopes of re-launching the peace process in the Middle East," said one. "Abbas was turning the Arafat page and opening new avenues for the future." But it forgets Abbas's own words according to which "a peace agreement with Israel will have to guarantee a sovereign Palestinian state within its 1967 borders and the East of Jerusalem as a capital". More significantly, the gap is widening between those who tell the newly elected president what he should do, and the harsh ground realities. The programme laid down by Bush for the new president stands within a three-point action list: fight terrorism; fight corruption; and reinforce democracy (that is, remove those who are not with "us"). Some would-be advisors also add the need to restore the economy – something that is actually more in the hands of the Israelis. How is it that nobody felt it necessary to add "putting an end to the occupation" and eventually making peace?

A reason is that the parties do not speak the same language. "A good Palestinian [National] Authority will not continue to use these Palestinians as pawns in a political struggle against the Jewish state by feeding fantasies that they will return to the pre-1967 Israel," writes Israeli Minister Natan Sharansky in the *Wall Street Journal*. "Instead, the free world should provide decent housing for those living in the camps," he adds. Sharon was quoted as saying: "The main action at this stage following the election should be Palestinian action on terror." Here is the point of a false logic made through assisting Palestinian reforms rather than resuming negotiations, and the underlying concept of the conference planned to take place in March in London. One thing to be done is deal with the pressing matters – restoring order, rationalising security services, integrating Hamas and re-launching the economy. Another is to look after the real issues: putting an end to the Israeli occupation, returning to pre-1967 borders, establishing a capital in East Jerusalem and defining a right of return for the refugees.

Abbas knows that he cannot impose any truce on militant organisations as long as the Sharon government does not put an end to targeted assassinations, incursions into Palestinian cities and occupation. These are the limits of his action, for everyone knows such decisions are in the hands of the Americans. Britain's *Financial Times* noted:

> To give the Israelis security and the Palestinians justice means a Palestinian state on nearly all the West Bank and Gaza with Arab East Jerusalem as its capital. The Sharon government believes the Gaza withdrawal will remove this prospect from the table. For Mr Abbas's election to mean anything, the US and their allies need to persuade Israel otherwise.

In Palestine, the world is not a stage. The footlights of the last campaign are now fading. The conditions for long-standing peace are widely known. The way to implement them isn't to go through the achievement of parallel demands based on a reciprocal agreement that never worked. They must be imposed by a representative international power, something the United States may do when they finally decide to take up their responsibilities. That would be far more concrete than any of those prevailing inane feelings of "peace and love" that are presently running on television shows. This is nothing but another smokescreen covering the infinite suffering of a population born to live in camps, and whose only hope would be to live in decent tents.

AMERICA MAY LOSE THE WAR ... OR MAYBE IT ALREADY HAS

31 JANUARY 2005

Last Sunday, the long-awaited elections sought by freedom's new crusaders confirmed something everybody knew. The Shiite population represents the majority in Iraq. What else? The Sunni community has been "democratically" sidelined, and even if some of them are being tempted to join the new constitution drafting process it is unlikely that they will be much representative of their community. And the future status of the Kurds remains unsolved. Although, according to press reports, these elections had "no legitimacy, no credibility, no democracy", they were supported by most of the neighbouring Arab countries, who feared the outbreak of civil war in Iraq, which could lead to partition. But isn't that where the country now seems to be heading? If the Sunni nationalists did not succeed in their attempt to derail the voting process, can the new Iraqi Shiite leaders govern the country by themselves? As for the occupation forces, United States President George W. Bush has just made clear that "they could stay at the same level at least until 2006". British Prime Minister Tony Blair used the bolder expression – that they would be withdrawn "as soon as possible". The reality is that nobody knows.

Actually, the Bush Administration may be in the process of losing the war in Iraq. And, at home, one wonders if it has not already lost it. First, on the ideological side, the neo-conservative vision behind the idea of invading and occupying an oil-rich Arab country that posed no threat to America is coming to light. The inanity of the "spreading freedom to the world" argument is now less accepted by an increasingly worried political class. The need for a nation and the availability of a local class of "democracy importers", to quote Professor Zaki Laïdi, are necessary elements for spreading democracy. None of this exists in Iraq. "No Iraqi regime will ever succeed if its political project is limited to keeping to the US pattern," Laïdi adds.

Second, on the military side, the level of troops has constantly increased to reach 150,000. But the results are the same. When Bush asked Congress to authorise an additional US$80 billion in excess of the budget last week, US Senator Edward Kennedy called it "a new 'Vietnamisation' process". The cost of both the invasion and occupation has now been estimated at US$250 billion – four times the amount experts had planned. This has started to make a growing number of American politicians uncomfortable, especially when the budget deficit already stands at US$418 billion.

Third, and more significant from a human point of view, the American population is getting tired. The 1400 or so US soldiers who have been killed in Iraq are weighing increasingly on troubled American minds. And those who have "just" been wounded, even more. But, according to US Defence Secretary Donald Rumsfeld, American soldiers wounded in this war have the highest chances of survival – 98 per cent. Improved protective equipment, coupled with the efficiency of the Forward Surgical Teams and Combat Support Hospitals, explain why whoever is not shot dead instantly has a greater chance of survival. Yet, irrespective of the quality of surgical institutions, wounded soldiers are a visible, lasting and negative manifestation of the war. The Bush Administration is doing whatever it can to hide the figures; wounded soldiers usually come back in the middle of the night at the Air Force's Andrews base, without any media coverage. But the growing number of wounded soldiers cannot be hidden forever. According to the Media Research Center of Los Angeles, quoted by the French daily *Le Figaro*, 2076 soldiers were wounded during the first nine months of the conflict, compared to 8296 during the 14 following ones. Television stations prefer not to show what could be seen as an "act of disloyalty", says the *Los Angeles Times*. But the mass-circulation newspaper *USA Today* published a front-page article two weeks ago that would have been inconceivable just six months earlier. Talking of the "American invasion", the daily reports in detail the complaints of the Iraqi Islamic Party, which had called for the boycott of the elections. These complaints included the removal of all former Baathists – and not just Saddam loyalists – from the government and the disbanding of the army; the building-up of new military bases feeding Iraqi suspicions that the United States want to stay and control Iraq's oil; the appointment of incompetent and corrupt administrators in the aftermath of Saddam's fall; and the failure to mobilise quickly for reconstruction. In conclusion, *USA Today* presented a Gallup poll showing that Americans are now equally divided between those who think that the number of troops in Iraq should remain at present levels; be reduced; be increased; or that the troops should be completely withdrawn.

It is unlikely that the Iraqi issue will be settled through military means. A political process based on eye-wash elections will not help either. The situation demands a complete change in thinking, including now the arbitrage of religious powers, as Bush's only answers are speculative threats against Syria and Iran. A recent trip to the United States confirmed that the population is getting increasingly nervous about contradictions within its country's foreign policy. How long will it take before this concern reaches Washington? Before he communicates with God, Bush should start listening to his people.

IRAQ'S WORSENING SITUATION MAY BE GOOD FOR PALESTINE

16 FEBRUARY 2005

Two years ago, the United States had already decided to go to war against Iraq. And yet it was making a show of diplomacy at the United Nations. Many observers believed then that US President George W. Bush would display some goodwill by re-launching the peace process in Palestine, in order to have freer hands in Iraq. That did not happen. The United States invaded Iraq and provided full support to the worst Israeli extremists. Now that the same Zionist neo-conservatives remain in command in Washington, why is the Bush Administration seemingly prepared to make a few sacrifices in Palestine? Because the situation in "democratic" Iraq commands it.

Further to so-called democratic elections – a fair illustration of community groups' ability to mobilise votes – Iraq continues on the path to insecurity and growing hatred against America. The elections looked like a wasted effort. They will not help to resolve any of the fundamental issues that the country faces, such as its national unity, its domestic security and the survival of any of its governments that will have to enforce its will at the point of the American gun. These elections had little to do with democracy. It all started with Bush's comment: "The world is hearing the voice of freedom from the centre of the Middle East." The world could not hear anything else, anyway, as the Iraqi truth was so obvious it had to be explained every day by dedicated columnists, in a rare example of conformist thinking. Observers had left the place open for lobbyists. Press syndicate Benador Associates led the way in promoting the official line. Amir Taheri, who made himself famous with his detailed assertions about Saddam Hussein's hidden weapons of mass destruction, made another hit. In an American boots-shining exercise, he described a "massive show of people power in one of the few genuinely clean elections ever held in any Arab country" (*Gulf News*, 3 February). Actually, these elections were "imposed on the opposition under the protection of military repression", as Sunni tribal leader Raad al Hamadani observed. The official US-appointed voting commission mentioned a figure of 54 per cent participation. Other sources (such as www.geostrategie.com) said that only one-third of eligible Iraqi voters could actually exercise their rights. No independent journalists were allowed to visit some areas. Television stations were authorised to film only five polling stations, four of them in Shiite areas. A mere 20 international observers were present, compared with the 2400 in Ukraine. "Elementary principles for an election were so little respected that [if these elections] had taken place in Syria or in Zimbabwe, the United States and the United Kingdom would have been first to denounce them," said Salim Lone, who served as communications director at the UN mission in Baghdad.

These days, it seems, democracy is no more about a government of the people by the people and for the people, but what is sought by America. Mahmoud Abbas's election was a "democratic" one, but Arafat's was not. However, Israel is the only democracy in the region that can maintain stockpiles of weapons of mass destruction because "it is not a threat to the US", as Bush's Senior Advisor Richard Bolton said. Opposition leader Ayman Nour is arrested in Egypt; detainees in Guantanamo Bay (Cuba) are stripped of their most basic rights; but this is democracy. Meanwhile, Bush's State of the Union address sticks to a pre-emptive doctrine and the continued presence of US forces in Iraq "as long as necessary"; US Secretary of State Condoleezza Rice confirms that attacking Iran is "a postponed decision that is not ruled out". One can feel the enthusiasm of the Arab people to whom Iraqi elections "put to rest the myth that Muslim nations are not ready for democracy" (*Gulf News*, 2 February). But one should be clear: democracy is not what suits a dominant power at a given time. Beyond a freely chosen effective government, Iraqi democracy should also deal with security and the rule of law, the treatment of minorities and, as British weekly *The Economist* reminded us, "the writing of a constitution that sets out the role of Islam, the balance between the centre and the provinces, and the sharing of oil revenues". Democracy has not yet won in Iraq, nor is it going to win if it tends towards a theocracy that the Unites States already said "it will not accept".

This worsening situation may lead the United States to move on Palestine, just to avoid being wholly cornered. The concept of a viable Palestinian state was re-affirmed by Bush and Rice, who told Israel to prepare for "difficult decisions". Then one will see what kind of pressure the United States can exert on Israel when it comes to hard facts. The Sharm Al Shaikh meeting, indeed, focused on security issues – those are the only ones of interest to Israeli Prime Minister Ariel Sharon.

"Bush has launched a global war on the grounds of morale at a time when the borders between war and peace are fading away," says analyst Alain de Benoit. And his moral war is endless. Why are so many countries in the region that were immune to terrorism 20 years ago now forced to face this new threat? Is it not because America perverted democracy through the use of selective definitions in order to extend its imperial grip? America's responsibility in the spread of Islamic fundamentalism should make democracy neophytes more cautious, as the results of Saudi elections in Riyadh show. "The battle to be led is not the one between good and evil, but a fight inside each of us between power and grace, cruelty and fraternity," writes French minister Dominique de Villepin in *Le requin et la mouette* ("The Shark and the Seagull", Plon Albin Michel, 2004). Will the Arab world accept as a perpetual destiny the control of a foreign power that tells it what to do? I believe not.

A CHANGE IN TONE WON'T DO THE TRICK

28 February 2005

When United States President George W. Bush arrived in Europe last week, some observers believed that the flag-waving crowds would welcome a repentant leader of the Free World. Bush would apologise for the disputes over Iraq with former allies. Europe and America would team up again and promote democracy in the Greater Middle East. "What unites us [is] stronger than what divides us." Before Bush could soften his tone, US Secretary of State Condoleezza Rice had paved the way with slogans such as "Let's work together" or "The time is now for diplomacy". Even Defence Secretary Donald Rumsfeld had to take back his comments about "old Europe". But the world has changed drastically in the past four years, and America's approach requires more than a mere change in style.

First, softened speeches are not enough to revive the transatlantic alliance. The prospect of a "strong Europe wished by America" and a "strengthened NATO relationship" will have done little to the new prevailing situation that could be summed up as follows: "Old Europe" is not doing that bad – as far as dynamism and the search for unity are concerned. And it even seems pretty young. In Brussels, Bush cannot have missed it. French President Jacques Chirac was present not only as a privileged guest at the first official dinner for the American President, but also as the most senior representative of the NATO Council. He was also the first of ten speakers of the European Union Council. More importantly, together with Belgian, Irish and German leaders – German Chancellor Gerhard Schroeder was entrusted with the Iran file – Europe spoke with one voice. "Europe doesn't split between new and old members but starts gathering around a co-divided project," Chirac said. "NATO is still the cornerstone of the transatlantic relationship," Bush answered. But Chirac stressed the increasing security role of the EU instead and backed Schroeder's call for a complete shake-up of the organisation. Italian Prime Minister Silvio Berlusconi made some noise as an uninvited

11th speaker. One hopes America has finally understood that it will never make it in Europe against France, Germany and many others.

Thus, changing the tone was not enough. But had the tone really changed? Europeans know the value of Rice's favourite arguments such as "Why should a unified Europe counterbalance the United States, since we share similar objectives?" Why, indeed, would Airbus manufacture aircraft when Boeing already makes them ... A symptomatic double-speak by America is apparent in an article by Ken Weinstein, Vice President of the neo-conservative think-tank Hudson Institute. The article was published by the French daily *Le Figaro* on the very day Bush, in an interview, was claiming his good faith towards Europeans. Talking about the Davos summit, Weinstein outlined British Prime Minister Tony Blair's and Chirac's comments about poverty in Africa, global warming and Aids. He observed: "Here is a glimpse of the transatlantic gap. Europeans raise serious questions, but secondary questions ...; the differences in tunes, of minds and of priorities between American and European leaders are striking." He went on to add that: "Slowly, the world's centre of gravity is shifting from the North Atlantic to the East." This is along the lines of the report "Mapping the global future" that was prepared by the CIA's National Intelligence Council (NIC) some months ago. It concluded that "Europe was not a power of the future" and thus, not something America should care about.

However, if one can say that Europe and America share the same values about democracy, freedom or international trade, what about Abu Ghraib, Guantanamo, the International Criminal Court of Justice or the Kyoto Protocol? Even though common views can be expressed or differences softened, Bush's basic line remains the same. "It's me against the world. And the good news is that the world is on my side – at least more than a half," as Dong Wead has just reported in *The Raising of a President* (Simon & Schuster, 2004) about the American president.[1] Is it worth it? Asked whether he would now invite Chirac to his ranch in Crawford, Texas, Bush answered: "I am looking for a good cowboy." Those attending said it was a joke.

As for Iraq, the epicentre of the regional earthquake ignited by the US President, it would be a mistake to believe Senator Joseph Biden when he says that "Bush is going to make it in Iraq and Chirac wants to have his share of it". Actual facts are hard to deny and what is happening in Iraq shows the point up to which US diplomacy should rebuild.

Thanks to America, Iran is finally winning its war against Iraq. Olivier Roy, an expert on Islam, describes the paradox created by Bush in the region: on the one hand, he helped Iran constantly in its ambition to become a regional power by destroying two of its fiercest enemies, Saddam Hussein and the Taliban – a combination of Baathists and Salafists, teaming up occasionally, as in Iraq today. On the other hand, the implementation of democracy has failed in Iraq because America did it in a technical and abstract way without giving enough consideration to the political legitimacy. In the Middle East, this can only come with nationalism and Islam. Only the Iraqi Shiites can now try to achieve it and the Bush Administration is left with very little choice but to oppose its own views about democracy, not to mention the feelings other American allies in the region have about such an outcome.

It is the true meaning of Rice's comment "there is no turning back". The United States can no longer support the dictatorial regimes that were supposed to maintain stability and give protection from Islamism. For the result of this policy is that religious leaders now emerged as those best protecting democracy. Europe might help America in tackling this paradox. But it goes far beyond the need "for a good cowboy".

NOTES

1   A former aide of President George H. Bush, Doug Wead sparked a scandal with his book because parts of it were extracts of conversations with then-Governor George W. Bush that were taped without their knowledge or consent.

TIME IS RUNNING OUT IN THE MIDDLE EAST

14 MARCH 2005

Once again, hands were shaken and pictures taken. One month ago, in Sharm Al Shaikh, the western press said peace would prevail, for they only like good news from the Middle East. If no bombs explode for some weeks, security is back; if Israeli Prime Minister Ariel Sharon and Palestinian National Authority President Mahmoud Abbas resume talking to each other, the peace process has nearly succeeded.

But why was it that there did appear to be some hope for the region this time? The death of veteran Palestinian leader Yasser Arafat was one of the reasons. But not because Arafat would have been an obstacle to peace and Abbas more committed to it. Abbas's political credo is the same as Arafat's and also the same as that of the majority of the Palestinian people. However, since both America and Israel had decided not to talk to Arafat any more, the election of Abbas changed the deal. Another reason was the apparent evolution of United States President George W. Bush with respect to the future of a viable Palestinian state. Whichever way the war is progressing in Iraq, things had begun to look encouraging. This being said, Sharm Al Shaikh's meeting was destined to delude from the outset.

The summit was dedicated to security issues that were only imposed on the Palestinians. No firm commitment was given by Sharon about the re-launching of the roadmap to peace. In Israeli eyes, terror has always been associated with the other side. And besides his personal interest in better controlling all Palestinian factions, Abbas's step-by-step approach could finally satisfy the Israelis. A kind of a ceasefire is a first mark along a road based on reciprocity. Abbas had little choice but to support the only available negotiation instrument. It stops short of solving any fundamental issues, but allows for a continued involvement of, and monitoring by, the international community. Finally, in so doing, Abbas showed his good faith to America, both in terms of controlling violence and his willingness to negotiate. If Sharm Al Shaikh can produce some positive results on daily issues that are of essence to the Palestinians – for example, free travel between Palestinian cities, and loosening the army's grip over the approximately 700 checkpoints spread over a territory of less than 5600 square kilometres – then maybe there is hope for the people. However, hard facts emerge against this positive scenario.

First, all history shows that no situation based on reciprocal agreement and parallelism ever worked in Occupied Palestine. The two peoples do not seem to have much to say to each other. The negotiation technique whereby major issues are kept until the end while small daily steps are made towards the other camp has failed. The widely agreed solutions to the conflict – a return to 1967 borders, two separate internationally recognised states, international status for Occupied Jerusalem and negotiated right of return for the refugees – cannot be implemented on a step-by-step basis, nor left until the end. They must be imposed by the international community – that is, America should exert pressure on Israel, simply because an insurmountable doubt would otherwise remain over whether the partners were both of good faith.

And this leads to a second reservation. Where is Sharon's good faith when he declares, as he did last week, that "Thanks to the settlements [colonies], we shall keep forever important positions that are essential to our existence, in [Occupied] Jerusalem, our unified capital forever, in the settlement [colony] blocks that are located in the most sacred parts of our history, and in the security zones that are of essence to our security"? The Israeli Knesset's Sasson report[1] has just evidenced the role of Sharon in the establishment of these 105 colonies that the Israelis themselves consider illegal. Sharon goes on building the wall, the result of which is to reduce the future Palestinian territory by nearly one-third of what it was supposed to be.

A third reason is the time the Palestinian people will be able to wait. Democracy was confirmed during the presidential elections, and more will follow with the next municipal and legislative elections in which Hamas said it will participate – providing, of course, the Israelis are prevented by the international community from disrupting them. Abbas was elected on the basis of the Oslo accords – that is, the belief that final peace would be reached as a result of small, positive events. Hence, he must deliver something to his people before other political groups make the people realise they did not receive anything concrete. Would a landside victory for Hamas in the summer help the peace process? Even though Abbas is said to be talking soon to Hamas leader Khalid Mishal in Yemen, the Americans should start thinking of it when they talk to Sharon.

Actually, the worst might be behind us. "What prevents us from moving forward is the present," said Leila Shahid, Palestinian representative in France. In other words, all the non-negotiable daily changes that Sharon pushes forward, making the situation irreversible, such as the reactivation of the Absentee Law, whereby Israel claims properties that it does not yet have, and the partition of Occupied Jerusalem, a place dear to followers of the three monotheistic religions and that some humans are now disfiguring with a wall that cuts across its face like a scar. How long will the people wait?

NOTES

1 On 18 March 2005, the Israeli parliament published a report prepared by MP Mrs Tania Sasson about the 105 illegal colonies set up in the Occupied Territories, and the role played by Ariel Sharon in these settlements. Following the conclusion of the Oslo Agreements, Israel undertook not to build any new settlements in the West Bank and the Gaza Strip. However, during the administration of Benjamin Netanyahu, the Israeli government began allowing the creation of outposts that had no official government approval, and were thus "illegal". In time, these outposts would become legalised or would be retroactively attached to an existing settlement. Sharon was involved in granting tacit approvals. Following the beginning of the second Intifada in September 2000, the creation of such outposts intensified. The Quartet roadmap peace process required that during the first phase, Israel would evacuate the outposts created after March 2001 (24 according to the Sasson reports). The future of the remaining 81 has been put in the hands of a "Special Committee" that has taken no decision to date.

THE BUCK STOPS WITH DAMASCUS

28 March 2005

France and the United States recently discovered that Syrian troops are still present in Lebanon. And they decided to join forces to pass resolution 1559 at the United Nations. The resolution calls for Syria's complete withdrawal from Lebanon, where it has maintained troops since the 1989 Saudi-sponsored Taif Accord which ended the Lebanese civil war. It also demands the disarming of the Shiite group Hezbollah. After the Taif Accord, Hezbollah was allowed to keep its arms in consideration of the role it played in freeing Lebanon from an Israeli occupation that lasted 22 years.

The motives of the United States President George W. Bush are clear. Syria, together with Iran, is one of the last Middle Eastern countries that refuses to bow to American pressure. The reason for invading Iraq was to change the balance of power in the region to the benefit of the United States and of Israel. But Syria remains an obstacle to that. Constantly trying to destabilise Syria has, therefore, been a policy of American neo-conservatives for the past few years. It is a way of punishing a country for the help it supposedly provides to the Resistance in Iraq. But the Syrians themselves seem not to be totally clear as to what they should do. The US policy also weakens Israel's most immediate enemy, now that Iraq has been "freed". Israel attacks Syria on the other flank. The campaign the Israeli government has launched against Hezbollah, the political ally of Syria in Lebanon, has never been so intense. It links Syria (and Iran) to "terrorism" and thus seeks to isolate the country further from the international community. The murder of former Lebanese Prime Minister Rafiq Hariri offered an opportunity to speed up the process.

Hariri's death meant more to France and its president Jacques Chirac. Hariri has been so generous with so many people during his life that his death was bound to leave a void. He blended personal interest with the Lebanese national economy – one may sneer at his company, Solidere, but one should not forget that Lebanon avoided a default on its

US$36 billion public debt mostly due to his creative debt management. But he had also become an unavoidable pawn on the Lebanese chessboard. By virtue of the Lebanese press that forgot the career and focused on the dramatic end, Hariri has become a martyr. For sure, his biggest achievement would have been to bring together the many segments of Lebanese society on the streets of Beirut. But what will happen next?

To start with and contrary to what many Lebanese think – notably the "Sister of the Martyr", Bahia Hariri – it is of limited importance to know who was behind the assassination. For once, the United States will not need to misrepresent the truth as it did with Iraq's weapons of mass destruction at the United Nations, simply because whoever did it, Syria is responsible for it, either because it was stupid enough to order it or because it could not prevent it. But, barring the possibility that hardliners plotted against Syrian President Bashar Al Assad, nobody sees how Syria could have done something that is so much against its own interest. This was neatly summed up by the Saudis: Syria being the dominant power in Lebanon, Hariri's murder means the Syrian security machine was either complicit in the crime or incompetent. One does not kill a politician, especially if he has the friends Hariri had. But other actors are now playing a risky game in this fragile environment.

If one excludes the dreams of the "Great Syria" or the absurd notion that one community can impose its rule over another, three major facts remain. First, Lebanon's mix of population has to live together. Each community must be recognised and the best way to do so is by not pitching one million people against another half million the following day. Ethnic or religious confrontations are not that old, as the recent bombings in Beirut have shown. Pointing the finger at Syria once again will not work, as nobody knows what might happen once violence erupts again. Second, geography and the interests of both countries demand that Lebanon cannot but have a special relationship with Syria, wherever Syrian troops are stationed. Business links between the various Lebanese communities and Syria run deep. Seeking another term for Lebanese President Emile Lahoud was surely a mistake. But to step up confrontation with Syria or to try to get rid of Hezbollah would only provoke further chaos. The Lebanese understand this and deemed it necessary to come to Paris last week and say it to Chirac. Finally, Lebanon (like Syria) shares a border with Israel. Damascus cannot stay indifferent to what is said about peace in the region. To forget Syria's strategic interest there would be foolish at a time when Phalangist leader Samir Geagea's followers demonstrate hand in hand with Druze leader Walid Jumblat's followers and others on the streets of Beirut. Lebanon can hardly forget that it was occupied for 22 years by Israel, whose present silence on the Lebanese issue is, incidentally, resounding.

Continuing to destabilise Syria as the United States and Israel seek to do will lead to revived tensions. Since Jordan is busy with American investors, the clues are in Syria. Once again, all roads eventually lead to Damascus.

SOWING THE SEEDS OF THE THIRD INTIFADA

11 April 2005

Israeli Prime Minister Ariel Sharon's Gaza evacuation plan is the "first concrete step towards peace", as some in the press have said. And he deserves unlimited support at a time when he is being subjected to fierce attacks. Sharon repeated this when he met United States President George W. Bush this week, during his 12th visit to Washington in just four years.

For the first time, Israel is going to release territories willingly and the decision by Sharon has provoked a flurry of insults and threats. The 7000 colonists who are going to be displaced after being paid hefty compensation had no right to be there in the first place. But United Nations resolutions regarding Israel have never been supposed to be respected, as the Iraqis and Syrians know. "The atmosphere looks very much like the one prevailing before [former Israeli Prime Minister] Yitzhak Rabin was murdered," warns the Israeli Ambassador in France, Nissim Zvili. Members of the extremist Kach movement make daily calls for a violent opposition to the dismantling of the colonies; injunctions are given by Rabbi Avraham Shapira to the soldiers not to rejoin their units after the Pessah holy day; even a *pulsa denura* or "evil spell" might be cast on Sharon by another Rabbi, Yossin Dayan, who made himself famous when casting such a spell on Rabin a few weeks before his assassination. So, is Sharon, who used to kill Palestinian civilians and was smart enough to sell America the concept of a link between terrorism and the Palestinian resistance after 9/11, another John Paul II? Nobody buys that.

First, some of the Israeli opposition to Sharon's policies is an internal affair that Sharon has to resolve by himself. It is a classic case of a minority that will exclude itself from democratic politics by continuing to reject the rule of the majority. The plan was passed in Parliament and all possible recourses were tried, but in vain. As happens in a democracy, the "only democracy of the Middle East" is that the minority has to abide by the wishes of the majority. Violent protests outside Parliament will provoke terrorism. The Israeli government must fight it with the same vigour it shows elsewhere. It is its responsibility and it does not seem to need any external help to do it. But will it be committed to doing so when, in the course of political meetings, it lets parliamentarians call Arabs "ramping worms", or people hold speeches as reported by French daily *Le Figaro*: "We cannot share this land with the Arabs. It is written in the Torah that we must expel them and if we cannot, then we should kill them"? Can one just reflect a second on the uproar a similar comment would have elicited around the world, if the word "Jews" had been substituted for the word "Arabs"?

But the worst is still to come. It appears that Sharon's move was purely tactical. While a pro-Israeli western press greets in advance the benefits of the Gaza evacuation, Likud never thought about hiding its true intentions. In November 2004, Dov Weisglass, Sharon's advisor, and then last month Sharon himself, openly announced that the evacuation was a kind of a trick to please the United States, so as to be able to do anything elsewhere. The Gaza colonies are just the tip of a scandalous iceberg, the occupation of Palestine by Israel. Attention is being diverted from what was supposed to be the next step – that is, the evacuation of 220,000 colonists from the West Bank. But Sharon will not even address the issue. Thanks to unlimited support from the United States, there were no United Nations sanctions imposed against Israel for not respecting resolutions passed against it. Going one step further, Bush admitted in April 2004 that "the US should acknowledge the demographic changes that occurred on the ground". The illegal colonies will thus be maintained; no territory will be made continuous for the Palestinians; occupation will go on in Jerusalem; and peace will be made impossible. But as former US Representative Paul Finley used to say (and as cited by Pascal Boniface in his book *Towards a Fourth World War?*) "The Middle East policy of the US is made in Israel and not in Washington." After last month's announcement of the creation of 3500 new units in Maaleh Adumin, another step towards linking Occupied Jerusalem to Israeli colonies, US Secretary of State Condoleezza Rice said: "These do not match with the American policy." Bush must have spoken the same language when he met Sharon this week. Sharon knows the combined strength of the Jewish lobby, the neo-conservatives and the Born Again Christians in the Bush Administration. He knows he does not need to worry.

On the ground, the situation is getting worse every day. In Bethlehem, the construction of the wall has cut off Occupied Jerusalem from the Arab side. The world is quietly witnessing a colonisation en-masse of an occupied land. Has the last Palestinian got to be expelled from Occupied Jerusalem for the world to start taking notice? When asked about all these actions that make peace even more distant, Ambassador Zvili answers: "One should not raise the questions for which there are no answers today." And all this while Mahmoud Abbas is losing credibility and Sharon believes time is working for him. Indeed, as Shakespeare said, "Time doesn't have the same appeal for every one."

MOMENT OF TRUTH FOR THE FRENCH

25 April 2005

On 29 May, the French will be given another chance to play one of their favourite games: voting No and thinking Yes. This is the date chosen by President Jacques Chirac for France to ratify the treaty signed by the representatives of the 25 states of the European Union in Rome on 29 October 2004. The treaty provides for a European constitution that will make Europe more democratic and efficient. Even though many of its 448 articles cover dispositions already in force, the four parts of the treaty include noticeable improvements. The Charter of Fundamental Rights is now included in the constitution, offering each European citizen full protection. The treaty also strengthens democratic controls. And for the first time, the principles of a social policy have been put on paper – a reason why Britain was hostile to it. A European foreign affairs minister will be elected; he will ensure Europe speaks in one voice and acts jointly in security affairs for which member states that are more advanced will be allowed to implement "strengthened co-operation", notably through the European Agency for Defence. The treaty is progressive despite being a compromise. It is another step towards giving political substance to an entity that would otherwise remain a minor political actor on the international stage. These are probably the reasons why, according to many polls, the French would vote against it.

In order to come into force on 1 November 2006, the treaty has to be ratified by all member states, either in parliament or through referendums. This exercise was supposed to be rather risk free. Spain (through a referendum), Italy and Greece have already passed the ratification Bill in parliament. In France, Chirac, under the disputable pretext that direct democracy would be more "democratic" for this important question than representative democracy, has chosen to seek ratification through the risky process of referendum. It is indeed dangerous in France, for the referendum has a long story of plebiscite behind it. In brief, people do not answer the question that is asked of them, but say "Yes" or "No" to the person who asks it; something rather irrelevant, as Chirac has already said he will not resign if the result is negative. And the French often lean towards the "No".

Listening to arguments from both sides confirms that only a few have actually read the treaty. It is not the case, however, of those politicians from both left (former Defence Minister Jean-Pierre Chevènement) and right (Philippe de Villiers and Jean-Marie Le Pen) who always opposed the idea of giving up a share of sovereignty. Giving up pieces of it surely has a price but other benefits tend to be forgotten – peace in Europe for the last 50 years, better living conditions, a growing role in world affairs. Actually, these people accept the concept of a strong European Union, provided it is managed by France. This is an interesting idea that, not surprisingly, was never bought by the other 24 members. They will therefore vote No, and they will make France split from its other partners. "We will renegotiate", they will then say. But with whom?

The other No-sayers include many different species: those who are hostile to government policies (such as the Trotskyites and what remains of the former communist party), and those with a personal agenda (former socialist Prime Minister Laurent Fabius). There's a few others, too, who don't understand easily – for instance, socialist MP Henri Emmanuelli or centrist MP Christine Boutin who, reading the same text, consider that voting Yes "would call the right of abortion into question" or "would allow homosexuals to adopt children".

At this stage, it is likely that the partisans of the ratification will have to gear up their message if they want to reverse the trend, as none of them are charismatic leaders. On top of that, Chirac made a poor presentation on a television show last week. Union for a Popular Movement (UMP) leader Nicolas Sarkozy could help, but seems to have been busier elsewhere, as if he anticipated a negative result. What a failed ratification would mean is still being debated. Maybe not the end of the world, but also surely not a stronger position for France in the European machinery. The No camp has no tangible alternative to propose. As French Prime Minister Jean-Pierre Raffarin said: "The Yes vote is a project, the No vote is a disorder." A No vote will be fatal to the European Union's ambitions to be a more global actor while the future of the euro, the only present tangible threat to American financial hegemony, will be doomed. The other European partners of France, Poland (probably) and Britain certainly expect that France will say No, so that they can torpedo a project that doesn't fit their transatlantic feelings. It may help to open the eyes of French voters who may finally prefer a non-perfect constitution to the risky uncertainties of the future. In this competition, some are prepared to play a leading role while others are paralysed by their own fear. It is up to France to say where she wants to stand.

EUROPE MUST COME TO THE AID OF SYRIA

9 May 2005

The shift in the traditional policy of France towards Syria cannot stop at the doors of the Syrian troops' withdrawal from Lebanon. The region merits a new set-up and the solutions may first be found in Damascus, not in Beirut.

On 27 April, the last Syrian troops left Lebanon, 30 years after they were invited by the Christian Lebanese to intervene militarily in the country. This period was marked by the deaths of 12,000 Syrian soldiers. An era finally came to an end. The 1989 Taif accords provided for the two countries to determine by themselves the size and duration of the Syrian presence in Lebanon, with the well-known positive effects on peace. But if Syria was allowed by the United States to retain its control over Lebanon at the time of the second Gulf War in exchange for a "positive attitude", the situation was to change in early 2003. Until that date, it was commonly assumed that a Syrian withdrawal was linked to a regional peace agreement. Yet French Foreign Minister Dominique de Villepin declared in April 2003 that: "It [is] necessary that as per United Nations Resolution 520, Lebanon recovers quickly its full independence and entire sovereignty." The Syrian accountability and Lebanese Restoration Act were passed by the US Congress in December 2003 and sanctions imposed in May 2004. United Nations Resolution 1559 gave an international legal framework to the process in September 2004, and the murder of Lebanese former Prime Minister Rafiq Hariri on 14 February was the final push that led to the resolution's implementation. "Lebanon has finally obtained the right to make its (own) political choices", Lebanese leaders now say, as if everything that went wrong in the country during the past several years was only the result of actions by foreign elements.

Syria should be praised for having shown respect for the United Nations resolution, but what should the next step be? It is indeed insufficient to portray Syria as an example for Israel in Palestine or the

United States in Iraq to follow, as these two countries don't really care about others' judgement.

One option is to focus on Lebanon. A new government is organising polls that are scheduled to take place next month. Time will then be available to assess the concrete achievements of the multi-confessional Lebanese crowds walking hand in hand in the streets of Beirut. General Michel Aoun is now back in business, waiting for Phalangist warlord Samir Geagea to be freed from jail and join the gang. As political leader Gassan Salamé said: "The Lebanese must show that they are able to govern by themselves." This goes beyond Lebanon's recurrent financial rescue in lieu of reforms and other Levantine political games. But other American cronies, swiftly joined by Israel, prefer to rush to a next step: the "normalisation" of Hezbollah and the signing of a peace treaty with Israel. "No Lebanese territories are any longer occupied by Israel," writes lobbyist Antoine Basbous, who complains about the "horrors" perpetrated by Hezbollah, such as "capturing three Israeli soldiers in order to exchange them for 430 Arab prisoners". Israel's ambassador in France, Nissim Zvili, was more direct: "Most Lebanese are fed up with the never-ending hostility towards Israel imposed on them by Syria and Hezbollah." Israeli Foreign Minister Sylvan Shalom said: "We hope the time has now come to make peace with Lebanon." Besides the disputed question of the Shebaa farms, can one seriously believe that peace can emerge as long as Israel, contrary to the United Nations resolutions, does not hand the Golan Heights back to Syria?

Another option is to look at Damascus, if only because Syria will never accept a regional loss of influence without reacting. A common view is that the Baath party in command is extremely undemocratic, inefficient and corrupt. The "Damascus Spring" did not survive a single year, and despite mixed signals the regime seems to be strengthening rather than loosening its grip over the country. Between the dreams of exiled intellectuals who believe in the benefits of free elections and the dark hopes of fundamentalists who resisted the slaughters in Hama in 1982, one fact remains: dictatorial regimes rarely tend to reform by themselves. Yet populations looking for greater freedom don't seem prepared to get it through America. Any positive international move on Lebanon should go hand in hand with a similar one towards Syria.

It could be two-fold. First, by bringing Israel and Syria back to the negotiating table. Syrian President Bashar Al Assad's last offers were bluntly rejected by Israeli Prime Minister Ariel Sharon. Israel may not want peace, as Sharon's attitude towards Palestinian President Mahmoud Abbas shows. But any attempt to isolate the Lebanese issue from the resolution of the Israeli–Arab conflict will lead to nowhere, as has been proved. Second, by convincing the Syrian government that the world has changed and that they could also take advantage of it. The country offers so many opportunities. Who can deny that Syria has a leading role to play? The United States will not accept this, but what about Europe and what about France? Irrespective of past disillusions, renewed efforts must be made. France may then change its policy on Syria, but this time for the better.

INDEX

A

Abbas, Mahmoud   31–4, 43, 46, 59, 187, 202, 205–6, 214, 221–3, 231, 239
Abdullah, Crown Prince (later King) of Jordan   116, 134
Abed Rabbo, Yasser   74
Abou Hanifa Mosque   25
Abrams, Elliot   29
Abu Dhabi   181–2
Abu Ghraib prison   129–33, 142, 196, 218
Abu Mazen *see* Abbas, Mahmoud
Acheson, Dean   53–4
Adler, Alexandre   53, 118
Adonis   43
Afghanistan   22, 37
Agency for International Development, US   29
Airbus (company)   37, 53, 81–2, 178, 218
Albright, Madeleine   100
Al Khobar   137
Allawi, Iyad   141, 145–6, 167–70, 192
Allen, Richard   177
Al Qaida   9, 21, 28, 41, 66, 75, 77, 85, 100, 115, 121, 137–8, 141–2
Alvineri, Shlomo   85
America-Israel Public Affairs Committee   134
Annan, Kofi   57–8
anti-Semitism   118–19, 163
Aoun, Michel   238
Arab American Institute   158
Arafat, Yasser   20, 31, 35, 50, 59, 65, 67, 75, 116, 118, 161, 171, 187, 214, 221
Armitage, Richard   86, 116
Asian tsunami   201–2
Al Assad, Bashar   96, 226, 238–9
Aventis (company)   53
"axis of evil" rhetoric   16
Azerbaijan   86

Aznar, Jose Maria   11, 35

B

Baker, Gerard   45
Baker, James   30, 90
Barhavi, Elia   74
Barnier, Michael   123, 159
Barry, Paul   26–7, 86
Basbous, Antoine   238
Bearing Point Inc.   29
Begin, Menachem   21, 65, 115
Beilin, Yossi   74
Ben Gurion, David   42, 115
Benador Associates   213
de Benoit, Alain   215
Berlusconi, Silvio   38, 46, 133, 217–18
Bethlehem   231
Biden, Joseph   165, 218
Bin Laden, Osama   16, 20–1, 33, 89, 100, 122, 126, 138–41, 150
Bin Sultan, Bandar   127
Blair, Tony   11, 23, 28, 33–5, 45, 66, 69, 82–3, 90, 95, 131, 150, 178, 195, 202–3, 209, 218
Boeing (company)   178
Bolton, Richard   214
Boniface, Pascal   2, 118, 126, 230
Bossi, Umberto   38
Boutin, Christine   234
Brahimi, Lakhdar   133
Bremer, Paul   58, 78, 87, 112, 134–5
Britain   9, 55, 82–3, 126–7, 202, 233–5
Brzezinski, Zbigniew   197
Bush, George senior   2, 99
Bush, George W.   2–3, 12–19, 23–7, 31–7, 41, 49–50, 54–79, 83–9, 95–100, 108, 113–50, 155–66, 174–81, 185–7, 192–6, 202–19, 225, 229–30
Bush, Laura   197
Buttiglione, Rocco   121

Bybee, Jay   142

C
Canada   100–1
Catholic Church   103–4
Central Intelligence Agency (CIA)   142, 145, 167, 218
Chaath, Nabil   188
Chalabi, Ahmed   27, 29, 122, 133, 145–6
Chechnya   174–5
Cheney, Dick   24–5, 74, 80, 99
Chevènement, Jean-Pierre   234
Chirac, Jacques   3, 23, 25, 33, 35, 50–1, 54, 59, 78, 123, 155, 167, 178, 182, 217–18, 225–6, 233–4
Clarke, Richard   121, 126
Clinton, Bill   141
coalitions of the willing   18
Cocteau, Jean   203
Cole, USS   16
Cooper, Richard   183–4

D
Dahrendorf, Ralph   193
Damascus   238
Dayan, Yossin   229
Debat, Alexis   36
debt   24, 26, 90, 225–6
democracy, nature of   137–8, 214
Dinoma   150
dollar exchange rate   183–4
domino effects   27
Donne, John   56
Duclos, Denis   59

E
Ebadi, Shirin   75
The Economist   187, 192, 195, 214
El Baradei, Mohammad   150
Emmanuelli, Henri   234
Erdogan, Recep   153
European Agency for Defence   233
European Bank for Reconstruction and Development   111
European Union (UN)   14, 28, 35, 46, 54–5, 70–1, 81–3, 89–91, 117, 122, 127, 153–5, 196–7, 217
    constitutional treaty   233–5

F
Fabius, Laurent   234
Fallujah   191–2
fanaticism   137–8, 151
Federal Bureau of Investigation (FBI)   196
Le Figaro   2, 96, 100, 210, 218, 230
Financial Times   30, 34, 45, 51, 63, 87, 95–9, 117–18, 122, 142, 161, 206
Finley, Paul   230
Fleisher, Ariel   41
Franklin, Benjamin   195
Franklin, Larry   165–6
Freedman, Lawrence   175
Friedman, Thomas   195
Fukuyama, Francis   104, 126

G
G8 summits   33, 111, 122
Gaddafi, Muammar   54, 97
Gardner, Jay   24
de Gaulle, Charles   21, 35, 42, 123, 170
Gaza Strip   117, 130, 133–4, 158, 161–3, 174, 187–8, 202, 229–30
Geagea, Samir   227, 238
Geneva Conventions   141–2, 163
Gillerman, Dan   134
Giscard d'Estaing, Valery   70
globalisation   201
Glucksmann, André   138
Golan Heights   32, 96, 238
Gonzales, Alberto   141–2, 196
Greece   233
Guantanamo Bay   79, 83, 86, 96, 100, 129, 142, 157, 196, 214, 218
Gulf News   2–3, 45, 116, 202, 214

H
Haaretz   202–3
Halliburton (company)   49, 78, 80, 99, 101
al Hamadani, Raad   213–14
Hama   238
Hamas   31, 41–2, 59, 65, 117–18, 125, 187–8, 202, 206, 222
Hariri, Bahia   226
Hariri, Rafiq   225–6, 237
Hass, Richard   158–9
Hassner, Pierre   83

Index

hegemony   13, 22, 53–5, 73–4, 82, 234
Hezbollah   26, 225–6, 238
Hifti, Nassi   42
Hiroshima   21
Hoagland, Jim   70, 196
Hollinger scandal   165
Holocaust, the   19
Hoon, Geoff   82
hostage-taking   169–71, 202
Hudson Institute   218
Hussein, Saddam   12–15, 23–7, 33, 38, 45, 50, 58, 69, 77, 79, 95, 99–100, 115–16, 122–3, 130, 133, 141, 146, 166, 191, 213, 219
Hussein Al Sad, Sheikh   166

I

Ignatieff, Michael   97
International Court of Justice (ICJ)   108, 149–50
International Criminal Court   142, 218
international law   19, 36, 45, 73, 78, 117–18, 142, 149–50, 161, 163
Iran   27, 37, 74–5, 86, 97, 111–12, 150, 196, 214, 219, 225
Iran-Contra scandal   147
Iraq War   2–3, 7–11, 15, 23, 33, 45, 49, 54, 73, 77, 81, 85, 95, 112, 157, 166, 185, 213, 225
Islam   8–9, 22, 104, 121–2, 157, 170, 214, 219
Israel   1–2, 19–23, 31–2, 42, 47, 50, 57–60, 66–7, 90, 96, 107–9, 113–18, 134, 149–51, 162, 173–4, 177, 188–9, 202–3, 214–15, 222, 225, 227, 230, 238
Italy   38, 45–6, 233

J

Jayousgota   90
Jerusalem   20, 74, 205–6, 222–3, 230–1
Jewish Institute for National Security Affairs   32
John Paul II, Pope   41, 96, 108, 174
Jordan   211
Jumblat, Walid   227
"just war" doctrine   7

K

Kagan, Robert   131
Karel, William   147
Kay, David   69
Kennedy, Edward   210
Kerry, John   2, 165–6, 177–8
Al-Khoï, Abdul Majid   28
Kissinger, Henry   31, 82–3
Kopchan, Charles   197
Krauthammer, Charles   126, 151, 178
Kristol, William   62, 101, 171
Kurds   24, 27, 154, 209
Kurtzer, Dan   46
Kyoto Protocol   218

L

Lacorne, Denis   62, 87
Lahoud, Emile   226
Laïdi, Zaki   209
Latiffya   167
Layne, Christopher   53–4
Lebanon   225–7, 237–9
Ledeen, Michael   32, 37, 39
Le Pen, Jean-Marie   234
Lewis, Bernard   62, 95, 151
Libya   112, 173
Lone, Salim   214
Los Angeles Times   210

M

McCleffan, Scott   118
McFarlane, Robert   16
McShane, Denis   38
Mahatir bin Mohamad   50
Maksoud, Clovis   111, 113
Marshall Fund   165–6
Mazuz, Menachem   141
Media Research Center, Los Angeles   210
Meir, Golda   42
Melloan, George   183, 196
Merkel, Angela   155
Metternich, Prince of   153
Michel, Louis   70–1
Mishal, Khalid   223
Mofaz, Saül   97, 112
Moïsi, Dominique   25, 170
Le Monde   2
money laundering   16

[243]

Montesquieu, Baron de 86, 104
Moore, Michael 146–7
Mortimer, Edward 58
Mubarak, Hosni 112
Mujahideen-e-Khalq 63–4
Murdoch, Rupert 13, 16
Muslim Brotherhood 30
Muslim headscarf issue 103–4, 169

N
Nassar, Sayed 89
Nasseriyah 121
National Security Council, US 99
Negroponte, John 130, 133, 146
Netanyahu, Benjamin 66
New York Times 162, 202
Niskanen, William A. 58–9
Nixon, Richard 141
Nokia (company) 53
North Atlantic Treaty Organisation (NATO) 14, 55, 81, 111, 158, 217
North Korea 95, 111
Northern Ireland 174–5
Nour, Ayman 214
Nye, Joseph 125

O
oil-for-food programme 23–5
oil resources 8
Olmert, Ehud 171
O'Neill, Paul 99, 126
Orwell, George 12
Oslo accords 20, 74, 222

P
Palestine 1–2, 7, 13, 19–22, 34, 38, 41, 46, 57–60, 67, 74, 108, 113, 116, 161–2, 174–5, 188–9, 202, 205–6, 214–15, 221–2, 231
Papacy, the 104
  see also John Paul II
Parmentier, Guillaume 14
Patten, Christopher 46
Peel, Quentin 74, 86, 97
Peres, Shimon 203
Perle, Richard 21, 26–32, 121, 134, 165, 174
Podhoretz, Norman 151
Poland 38, 70–1, 90–1, 165, 197, 234–5

Politique Internationale 3, 101
Powell, Colin 16, 20, 29, 58, 66, 95–6, 100, 126, 130, 134, 149, 202
"pre-emptive war" doctrine 25, 45, 53, 214
Putin, Vladimir 174

Q
Qorei, Ahmed 108, 117, 187
"Quartet" group 31, 34, 59
Qur'an, the 22

R
Raffarin, Jean-Pierre 234
Al Rantissi, Abdulaziz 42, 125
Record, Jeffrey 100
Red Cross 196
refugees 20, 46, 206, 222
Reinhart, Tanya 20
religious freedom 103–4
Rice, Condoleeza 3, 33–4, 41, 45, 66, 69, 73, 130, 193–6, 214–19, 230
"Roadmap" peace plan 31–2, 35, 38, 41, 50, 59, 66–9, 108, 126, 129–30, 162–3, 188–9, 203, 221
Robespierre, Maximilen 173
Ross, Dennis 161–2, 188
Roy, Olivier 62, 219
rule of law 117, 146, 214
Rumsfeld, Donald 15, 21, 25, 30, 38, 49, 74, 62, 70, 77, 81, 83, 130, 142–3, 165–6, 210, 217
Russell, Lord John 135

S
Sachs, Jeffrey 73, 142
Al Sadr, Moqtada 121, 166–7
Saint Malo declaration (1998) 82
Salamé, Ghassan 62–3, 238
Sarkozy, Nicolas 234
Sasson Report (2005) 222
Saudi Arabia 8, 137, 139, 215
Schroeder, Gerhard 35, 51, 54, 78, 178, 217
Seale, Patrick 86, 202
secularism 104–5, 154
Senor, Dan 141
September 11th 2001 attacks 16, 19, 22, 73, 77, 125, 139, 150–1, 158, 166, 174, 178

INDEX

US Congressional Commission on 141
Shahid, Leila 223
Shakespeare, William 36, 231
Shalom, Avraham 107
Shalom, Sylvan 163, 238
Shapira, Avraham 229
Sharansky, Natan 206
Sharm Al Shaikh meetings
  November 2004 191, 215
  February 2005 221–2
Sharon, Ariel 8, 13, 20–1, 29–34, 42–3, 46–7, 50, 63–9, 74–5, 96, 107–9, 116–19, 125–6, 130–41, 149–50, 157–66, 187–8, 202–6, 215, 221–3, 229–31, 238–9
Siegman, Henry 109
Sistani, Ali, Ayatollah 121, 167
Sivan, Erfal 119
Sloterdijk, Peter 73–4
"soft power" 125
Spain 70–1, 75, 90–1, 115, 197, 233
Spiers, Ronald 158
Stalin, Josef 174
Steinberg, Gerald 46–7
Stephens, Philip 18, 27, 32, 35, 55, 70, 79, 96, 134, 155, 161, 178, 193
Stern, Jessica 59
Straw, Jack 97
Sudan 95
Suez crisis (1956) 8
Swift Boats Veterans for Peace 166
Syria 27–32, 69, 74, 86, 111, 211, 225–7, 237–8

T

Taheri, Amir 3, 25, 37, 85, 101, 213
Taif accords 225, 237
Taliban forces 141–2, 219
Telhami, Shibley 158
terrorism 20–1, 27–30, 37, 41–2, 57, 59, 73, 78–81, 85–6, 96–100, 108, 112–16, 121, 126–7, 134–5, 138–9, 151, 166, 170, 173–5, 215
torture 142–3
Turkey 153–5, 165

U

United Arab Republic (AUR) 181–2
United Council for Iraqi Resistance 146

United Nations 12, 17, 20, 26, 57–8, 62–3, 70, 78, 96, 112, 116, 122–3, 126, 130, 163, 174, 201–2, 213, 226
  Resolutions 7, 23, 65, 75, 108, 116, 118, 134, 145, 149, 229–30, 237–8
  Security Council 7, 11, 26–7, 96
  weapons inspectors 11, 26
USA Today 210–11

V

Vanunu, Mordechai 150
Védrine, Hubert 20, 71, 178
Vichy regime 35
Vietnam War 81, 173–4
de Villepin, Dominique 17, 32, 58, 61–2, 112–13, 121, 123, 215, 237
Villiers, Philippe de 234

W

Walesa, Lech 75
Wall Street Journal 7, 12, 25, 30, 34, 37, 45–6, 49–50, 62, 66, 75, 78, 90, 96, 108, 117–18, 122, 129, 142–3, 165, 169, 191–2, 196
Wead, Dong 218
weapons of mass destruction 11, 23, 26, 29–30, 41, 45, 69, 77, 79, 85, 89, 95, 97, 100–11, 115, 121, 141, 150, 158, 166, 213–14, 226
Weinstein, Ken 218
Weisglass, Dov 188, 202–3, 230
Wilde, Oscar 99
Wolf, Martin 12, 34, 46, 97
Wolfowitz, Paul 25, 27, 30, 62, 77, 90, 111, 134
Wolsey, James 32
Woodward, Bob 125–7
World Trade Organisation 111

Y

Ya'alon, Moshe 30, 117
Yanbu 137
Yassin, Sheikh 38, 117

Z

Zayed Bin Sultan Al Nahyan, Sheikh 181–2
Zionism 109, 150, 174, 213
Zvili, Nissim 229, 231, 238